THE
JEW *and*
PALESTINE
IN
Prophecy

M. R. DeHaan, M.D.

Zondervan Publishing House
GRAND RAPIDS, MICHIGAN

INTRODUCTION

There are two lines of redemption which run parallel and unbroken throughout the Scriptures. The first is the line of personal redemption, or individual salvation for the sinner. God declared His provision for this personal redemption of the sinner in the first promise to man in Genesis 3:15, and demonstrated it in the first sacrifice in Genesis 3:21. From there throughout the entire Scriptures God reveals progressively how the sinner must be saved by grace through faith in God's own substitute. In the Old Testament it was revealed in type. In the New Testament we have a full revelation in the death and resurrection of Jesus Christ.

There is another aspect of redemption which also runs in an unbroken line throughout the Word of God. After man had failed in his own government, God gave up the nations of the world, and chose Abraham to become the father of one favored nation, through Isaac and through Jacob. This nation was the nation of Israel. God chose the Israelites to be His people, to lead all the rest of the nations to Him in the end time. However, Israel failed, and when the Messiah came nineteen hundred years ago to offer the ideal Messianic Kingdom to the nation of Israel, they refused their King, the kingdom was set aside for the present, and God's line of personal redemption only continues during this dispensation "until the fulness of the Gentiles be come in."

During this age, therefore, Israel, the kingdom nation, is in trouble, scattered and persecuted among the Gentiles, but although scattered and passing through the fires of affliction, she cannot be destroyed, for God's promise still stands sure. Israel's history divides itself into three periods, past, present and future. In the past she was blessed in the land, but rebelled against Jehovah. In the present she is scattered and persecuted, but supernaturally preserved. In the future she as a nation shall be fully restored in the glory of the kingdom here upon the earth.

This truth is not only taught in Scripture by clear, direct prophecies, but also revealed in a number of graphic figures. The burning bush in Exodus three is a picture of Israel burning, burning in the desert of the nations, but never to be destroyed. The vine of Isaiah five is another figure of Israel, unfruitful for a time, but one day to blossom and bud and fill the face of the earth with fruit. The fig tree also is another figure of Israel, cursed from the roots and withered, but some day to bud again. In the same way, the olive tree of Romans eleven is the nation of Israel, her branches cut off for a time, but only to be grafted in again when the fullness of the Gentiles be come in. The same truth is taught in the vision of the dry bones and the two sticks of Ezekiel thirty-seven.

In this volume we shall study some of these prophetic visions and figures to demonstrate the harmony of God's Prophetic Word, and the certainty of the fulfillment of all prophecy. The messages deal largely with Israel as a nation, her present distress and her future restoration. It is the firm conviction of the author of this volume that unless we learn to distinguish between Israel and the Church, the bulk of prophecy must remain unintelligible. The key to the proper understanding of the Word of God in all of its fullness consists in distinguishing between the line of personal redemption and the line of earth's redemption at the Second Coming of Jesus.

To mix Israel and the Church, to make the Church spiritual Israel, is the surest way to bring upon one's self the very blindness which characterizes natural Israel today (Romans 11:25). It is with a hope the reader may learn to distinguish the things that differ that these chapters are sent forth. We must be able to distinguish law and grace, Israel and the Church, the Kingdom and the Body of Christ. Failure to do this limits our Bible by making whole sections and even whole books practically worthless, except for moral applications and instructions, while leaving us entirely in the dark concerning God's Prophetic Kingdom Program at the consummation of the ages.

These messages were first given over the coast-to-coast broadcast of the Radio Bible Class, and are printed in this form in answer to many requests to have these lectures in one single volume. They are printed almost in the identical form in which they were given over the air. With a prayer that these simple studies may be as abundantly blessed as they were when first broadcast over the air, we send this book forth to the glory of God and for the comfort of God's people.

M. R. De Haan

TABLE OF CONTENTS

Chapter One

DRY BONES

The hand of the Lord was upon me, and carried me out in the spirit of the Lord, and set me down in the midst of the valley which was full of bones,

And caused me to pass by them round about: and, behold, there were very many in the open valley; and, lo, they were very dry.

And he said unto me, Son of man, can these bones live? And I answered, O Lord God, thou knowest.

Again he said unto me, Prophesy upon these bones, and say unto them, O ye dry bones, hear the word of the Lord.

Thus saith the Lord God unto these bones; Behold, I will cause breath to enter into you, and ye shall live:

And I will lay sinews upon you, and will bring up flesh upon you, and cover you with skin, and put breath in you, and ye shall live; and ye shall know that I am the Lord.

So I prophesied as I was commanded: and as I prophesied, there was a noise, and behold a shaking, and the bones came together, bone to his bone.

And when I beheld lo, the sinews and the flesh came up upon them, and the skin covered them above: but there was no breath in them.

Then said he unto me, Prophesy unto the wind, prophesy, son of man, and say to the wind, Thus saith the Lord God; Come from the four winds, O breath, and breathe upon these slain, that they may live.

So I prophesied as he commanded me, and the breath came into them, and they lived, and stood up upon their feet, an exceeding great army (Ezekiel 37:1-10).

THIS PROPHECY, GIVEN BY VISION to the prophet Ezekiel over 2,500 years ago, is in the process of fulfillment before our very eyes today. The recent events in the land of Palestine with the political restoration of the nation of Israel is a direct and unmistakable fulfillment of that which Ezekiel beheld in the vision of dry bones, and heralds the soon return of the Head of the Church and the Messiah and King of Israel, Jesus Christ. Among all the signs of the times there is none more clear than the political re-establishment of the nation of Israel in the land of Canaan. If there is one thing clear in the Bible, it is the revelation that the nation of Israel, the Twelve Tribes of Jacob, will in the end time be re-gathered into the promised land, delivered forever from their wanderings and oppressions. It is taught in a thousand clear and unmistakable prophecies, and predicted in type and symbol throughout both the Old and the New Testaments.

THE BIBLE IS FULL OF ISRAEL'S RESTORATION

Time would utterly fail us to repeat the many, many promises of this event in the Bible. We mention only a few before we take up the subject as it is revealed in the vision of the valley of dry bones. Way back in the book of Leviticus, before Israel had even entered the land of promise, God had already predicted its future.

> And I will scatter you among the heathen, and will draw out a sword after you: and your land shall be desolate, and your cities waste.
> And upon them that are left alive of you I will send a faintness into their hearts in the lands of their enemies; and the sound of a shaken leaf shall chase them; and they shall flee, as fleeing from a sword; and they shall fall when none pursueth.
> And ye shall perish among the heathen, and the land of your enemies shall eat you up.
> And they that are left of you shall pine away in their iniquity in your enemies' lands; and also the iniquities of their fathers shall they pine away with them (Leviticus 26:33, 36, 38, 39).

Or consider carefully the words of Moses given in Deuteronomy:

> And the Lord shall scatter thee among all people, from the one end of the earth even unto the other; and there thou shalt serve other gods, which neither thou nor thy fathers have known, even wood and stone.
>
> And among these nations shalt thou find no ease, neither shall the sole of thy foot have rest: but the Lord shall give thee there a trembling heart, and failing of eyes, and sorrow of mind:
>
> And thy life shall hang in doubt before thee; and thou shalt fear day and night, and shalt have none assurance of thy life:
>
> In the morning thou shalt say, Would God it were even; and at even thou shalt say, Would God it were morning! for the fear of thine heart wherewith thou shalt fear, and for the sight of thine eyes which thou shalt see (Deuteronomy 28:64-67).

Surely no one can deny that this is the most accurate description of the entire history of the persecuted nation of Israel for the past three thousand years of her history. When we realize that this accurate and detailed description was written before Israel was even a nation in the land of Palestine, one cannot doubt the infallibility of this wonderful Book. Who else could have depicted the entire course of this nation's history but omniscient God Himself! For twenty-five hundred years this people has been scattered among the nations, maligned, persecuted, hated and tortured, under Nebuchadnezzar, Alexander, Antiochus, the Caesars, under Russia, Hitler and Mussolini. At one time they were reduced in number to less than one million, and we are told that eight million perished under the godless regime of Hitler alone.

PROPHECIES LITERALLY FULFILLED

We might multiply a thousand such prophecies in the Old Testament, every one of which was fulfilled to the very letter. What right then has any one to deny the prophecies written at the same time by the same men which deal with the literal restoration of this same nation? Common sense alone and integrity of interpretation demand that the unfulfilled prophecies concerning the nation of Israel must be as literally fulfilled as the prophecies which have already come to pass. If the predictions of Israel's scattering among the nations were literally fulfilled, I submit to you that the predictions concerning its re-gathering must be just as literally fulfilled, if we are to deal honestly with the Word of God.

ISRAEL IS TO BE LITERALLY RE-GATHERED

Consider, therefore, the Word of God with regard to Israel's future, remembering that God's Word concerning its past was fulfilled to the letter. We might quote hundreds of passages, but here are a few.

> And yet for all that, when they (Israel) be in the land of their enemies, I will not cast them away, neither will I abhor them, to destroy them utterly, and to break my covenant with them: for I am the Lord their God (Leviticus 26:44).

Or consider this passage also given long before Israel had even been driven from the land among the nations; in fact, before it had even entered the land of promise.

> And it shall come to pass, when all these things are come upon thee, (the things predicted concerning their scattering among the nations) the blessing and the curse, which I have set before thee, and thou shalt call them to mind among all the nations, whither the Lord thy God hath driven thee,
>
> And shalt return unto the Lord thy God, and shalt obey his voice according to all that I command thee this day, thou and thy children, with all thine heart, and with all thy soul;
>
> That then the Lord thy God will turn thy captivity, and have compassion upon thee, and will return and gather thee from all the nations, whither the Lord thy God hath scattered thee.
>
> If any of thine be driven out unto the outmost parts of heaven, from thence will the Lord thy God gather thee, and from thence will he fetch thee:
>
> And the Lord thy God will bring thee into the land which thy fathers possessed, and thou shalt possess it; and he

will do thee good, and multiply thee above thy fathers
(Deuteronomy 30:1-5).

If these words do not mean the literal, national re-
gathering of the nation of Israel in Canaan, then the
Bible becomes an unintelligible Book and all Bible reading
or study becomes a senseless waste of time. If the predictions given in Deuteronomy twenty-eight and twenty-
nine concerning Israel's dispersion, were literally fulfilled,
then common sense demands that the predictions concerning their restoration in this chapter must just as literally
be fulfilled.

HISTORY STANDS AS PROOF

All history stands as proof of the literal fulfillment of
the Word of God. Israel has been scattered among the
nations, but never destroyed. For millenniums it has been
scattered like leaves, among the Gentiles, yet never losing
its identity, because God preserved it for the fulfillment
of His promise to re-gather the nation in the end time, and
make it the nation of God's kingdom upon the earth. Today
we stand at the very threshhold of the fulfillment of these
prophecies. Few people realize the importance of the recent developments in Palestine. The most outstanding and
significant sign of the fulfillment of prophecy, outshining
all others, is the political recognition of Israel as a nation
in the land of promise. It outshines all other events. We
are witnessing today the fulfillment of prophecy in the
increase of wickedness predicted for the end time, the
moral decay, wars and rumors of wars, earthquakes, race
hatred, the revival of the Roman Empire in the countries
about the Mediterranean Sea, the rise of the Northern
Confederacy and her satellites, the discovery of the atomic
bomb. All these are significant fulfillments of the Word of
God, all of them having been foretold. However, none of
them can compare with the significance of the revival of
the State of Israel. Think of it! For the first time in
2,500 years Israel is recognized by the world as a nation in

her own right, with her own constitution, army, navy, her own flag, her own currency, recognized by the other nations. Remember, for 2,500 years they had no national existence in their land, but today, in our own generation, we are witnessing the beginning of the fulfillment of prophecy, when a "nation shall be born in a day." The dry bones have begun to move. The dry bones are coming together and sinews and flesh have formed upon the skeleton of the nation of Israel, and the skin which binds the nation together is clothing them. Only one more thing remains, the breath of the Lord entering them and the resultant spiritual revival and the recognition *By God* of the nation of the covenant in the land of their fathers.

THE VALLEY OF DRY BONES

All of the above is according to prophecy and according to plan. There are many, many figures in prophecy which give us this same picture. The burning bush in the desert represented Israel in the fires of affliction, but never to be consumed. The vine of Isaiah five is a picture of Israel, the vineyard of the Lord given over to her enemies, but some day to be restored and revived. The fig tree which Jesus cursed is the same picture, withered *from* the roots, only to blossom and bud again some day as a sign of the end of the age. The fig tree is budding today and blossoming once more in the land of Palestine. There is as yet no fruit, but that will follow soon. The same truth is expressed by Paul in Romans by the figure of the olive tree, whose branches (Israel) are broken off temporarily while God deals with the Gentiles, but some day they too are going to be grafted in again. The grafting seems to be going on at this very moment. In this same vein Ezekiel was given the vision of the valley of dry bones, and we know that it represents the nation of Israel, for Ezekiel is told in chapter thirty-seven:

> . . . these bones are the whole house of Israel: behold,
> they say, Our bones are dried, our hope is lost: we are

cut off for our parts.

Therefore prophesy and say unto them, (Israel) Thus saith the Lord God; Behold, O my people, I will open your graves, and cause you to come up out of your graves, and bring you into the land of Israel.

And shall put my spirit in you, and ye shall live, and I shall place you in your own land (Ezekiel 37:11, 12, 14).

This in broad outline is God's program for Israel, taking shape right now and in the process of fulfillment before our very eyes. In the following chapters we shall see the steps by which Ezekiel sees this prophecy being fulfilled. A careful reading of Ezekiel thirty-six and thirty-seven, before reading the next chapter will greatly help in understanding this remarkable prophecy of Israel's restoration taking place at this very moment in these closing days.

Soon the King will come, and the fulfillment will be complete. Israel as yet has no king. Israel is a democracy, not a kingdom. For this reason Palestine and Israel have a president but no king. When the Lord comes, David shall be their king, and Christ shall be King over all the earth.

The next event is the coming of Israel's Lord, and King, to settle the nation forever in the land. As we see these tremendous events we can lift our voices with John in Revelation, "Even so, come, Lord Jesus."

Chapter Two

ISRAEL AMONG THE NATIONS

IN THE THIRTY-SEVENTH CHAPTER of Ezekiel the prophet is carried away in a vision to a great valley filled with bones and these bones were very dry. Then he is told to prophesy to these bones and as he does, there is a noise among the bones, then a shaking, next a movement of the bones, then each bone moves to its own adjacent bone, then flesh and sinews finally clothe the restored skeleton and skin covers them about, but the body is still dead; there is no spirit in it. Again the prophet is commanded to prophesy to the wind, and as he does so, life enters into the bodies, they move, they breathe, they arise and stand upon their feet.

The interpretation of this vision is given in the verses which follow. Yet it is one of the strangest things that only a few who seem to study their Bibles take this divine interpretation seriously. As I prepared these chapters I turned to and read a great many commentaries written by many great theologians and scholars just to see what added light they could throw on the subject. I finally gave up in utter disgust after reading one interpretation after another and found that almost all of them ignored God's own interpretation and insisted upon spiritualizing this vision and making it to apply to the church, or to the individual, or our own nation. Such is the deception of

spiritualizing the Scriptures, instead of reading them literally as God intended us to.

To be sure, the vision of the valley of dry bones is a
figure, but it is a figure of a literal thing and this is
certainly not the church, the individual, or the nations
of the world. Beautiful applications are made to the
church, comparing it to a valley of dry bones and in
need of a revival. It may make a good revival sermon, but
it utterly ignores the primary meaning and purpose of
this vision. There is absolutely no excuse for such dealing
with the Bible when the key to the meaning hangs right
by the door. The Lord Himself interprets this vision for
us. Listen to it:

> Then he said unto me, Son of man, these bones are
> the *whole house of Israel*: behold, they say, Our bones are
> dried, and our hope is lost: We are cut off from our parts.
> Therefore prophesy and say unto them, Thus saith the
> Lord God; Behold, O my people, I will open your graves,
> and cause you to come up out of your graves, and bring
> you into the land of Israel.
> And ye shall know that I am the Lord, when I have
> opened your graves, O my people, and brought you up out
> of your graves.
> And shall put my spirit in you, and ye shall live, and
> I shall place you in your own land: then shall ye know that
> I the Lord have spoken it, and performed it, saith the Lord
> (Ezekiel 37:11-14).

There is the proper interpretation of the vision of the
valley of dry bones, according to the Word of the Spirit
of God Himself. The key hangs right by the door and
its meaning is simple, clear and easy to understand.
Here are the words again, "These bones are the *whole
house of Israel.*" They are scattered today throughout the
valley of the nations and are in the place of death, nation-
ally. For centuries and millenniums they are out of
Canaan, without a national existence, recognition, a national flag or government. But, says the prophet way
back there over twenty-five hundred years ago, there

is a time coming when these bones, the nation of Israel, shall be gathered and spiritually resurrected, and go back into *their own land*. This is God's own interpretation of the vision of the valley of the dry bones.

Having seen that the dry bones are the whole house of Israel, we now can interpret the various details given in this chapter. A number of things are emphasized:

1. These bones are very dry.
2. These bones are in the open valley.
3. There are very, very many of these bones.

In the light of God's own interpretation these details are not hard to understand. The open valley refers to the nations of the world. Among these Israel has been scattered for over 2,500 years. Significantly, it is called a valley and not a mountain top. A valley suggests shadows and darkness. When we speak of sorrow, we call it the Valley of Sorrows; when we talk of death, we speak of the Valley of the Shadows. And the place of these bones in the valley is strikingly descriptive of Israel's sad history. Truly it has been a history of shadows, beginning with their affliction under Pharaoh in Egypt all through the centuries until this very day.

Very Many in Number

Next we are told the bones are *very* many in number. Eternity only will reveal the countless hundreds of millions of Israel's nation who have perished among the nations since the days of Moses and Egypt. Any attempt to calculate the number would be pure guesswork. Millions were slain in Russia alone within the last century. Eight million died under the devilish reign of Hitler alone in Germany. There is not a nation on the face of the earth, hardly a square mile of the inhabited earth, where the bleaching bones of Israel's race cannot be found. Indeed, they are very many.

They Are Very Dry

Next we are told that these bones are very dry. Not merely dry, but *very* dry. This suggests, of course, that they had lain there for a long, long time. They were not green bones, but they were very dry. For centuries and millenniums Israel has been scattered among the nations, out of their own land, pining in the open valley of the nations. It also suggests hopelessness, and absolute death, and will require a miracle of resurrection by Almighty God. No wonder, then, that the question is asked of Ezekiel, "Can these bones live?" That is the question which has been asked a thousand times since then. As we look upon the nation of Israel, her national existence in the land interrupted for all these centuries, her tribes scattered throughout the world, the question may again be asked. Is there any hope for the nation of Israel? Will they ever be restored again to the land of their fathers, and will they ever again see the glory of the Kingdom of Israel as they saw it under King David and Solomon? Many answers have been attempted. Our text tells us what Israel herself says in answer to this question. In verse eleven it is made to say:

> Our bones are dried, and our hope is lost: We are cut off from our parts.

The restoration of Israel after all these years seems impossible even to the nation itself, and there are thousands of the seed of Jacob who have given up all hope of ever being restored as a nation to the land again. The same error is made by a host of professing Christendom, who flatly deny that Israel will ever be literally restored as a nation to the land, to set up the Kingdom of the Messiah. In order to get around the plain teaching of the Scriptures these people resort to the interpretation of Scripture which is usually called "spiritualizing." By this method all the prophecies concerning Israel are applied to the church, which is then called spiritual Israel. Therefore most people believe that God is all done with Israel as a nation. The Jews can be saved as individuals just as any one else, but as to any national restoration, they say that is hopeless and will never occur. We are not surprised that prophecy to these folks is a closed book and they seldom attempt to interpret it. Whole sections of the Word of God are blocked off by this method of spiritualizing and seldom referred to or considered. In many many circles, therefore, the truth of Christ's Second Coming, the restoration of the Jews, the setting up of a millennial kingdom on earth, is never taught or even mentioned, in spite of the fact that the Bible is full of it from cover to cover.

In the resurrection of these dry bones of the house of Israel there are two distinct stages. The prophet is commanded to prophesy *twice*. When he speaks the first time five things happen, as follows:

1. There is a noise among the bones.
2. There is a shaking of the bones.
3. There is a moving of bone to bone.
4. Flesh and sinews appear on the skeleton.
5. Skin covers the body.

Notice that all this happens without a breath of life entering this restored body. While bone has come to bone and the body is organized into its complete form, there is still no life. It is not until the prophet is told to prophesy to the wind, and commands breath to enter this body, that life appears and the bodies stand upon their feet, an exceeding great army. It is of the utmost importance that we recognize this twofold response to the Word of the Lord. The first stage has already happened. Israel has been re-gathered in part at least in Palestine, and the body of the nation is organized. But the return has been thus far only *political* and not *spiritual*. The spiritual revival will not come until the Messiah King appears upon the scene.

First a Noise

The very first thing mentioned is a noise among these
dry bones. It is the sound of sorrow and of woe. It
is the cry of Israel's wailing wall which has ascended unto
God since the days of their bondage under Pharaoh until
this day. Their cry is being heard. We believe the noise
among the bones refers especially to the cry of millions of
the sons of Jacob within the past generation. Never before
in all of history has Israel passed through the fire of persecution as in recent years, with millions banished from
their homes, left to die in prison camps, shot down like
animals, and denied refuge in the greater part of the
earth. Yes, there has been a noise of distress among the
bones as never before.

A Shaking and a Moving

Following the *noise* comes the shaking and the moving
of the bones. They are moving toward one another, bone
to bone. As a result of the recent persecutions there has
arisen a new national consciousness in Israel and many
movements were organized to restore the Jews again to
their own land. Notable among these was the Zionist
movement, with the one single purpose of repossessing
Palestine as their national home land. Instead of pur-
suing their activities in the different nations more or
less independently, they have come to realize a common
need and have united in the common aim to return to their
own land.

Sinews, Flesh and Skin

Next sinews and flesh come upon the reconstructed
skeleton. Muscles and sinews in the body speak of co-
ordination, unity of action, purpose and strength. As a result of the various movements among Israel's sons in the
past generation, the nation has been reborn. They have
organized as a nation in the land of Palestine, and the
sinews and flesh are already upon the skeleton of the new
nation. One more thing is mentioned. Skin now appears

and clothes the body. Skin is the protection of the bones, the muscles, the sinews and the other tissues, against injury from without. This too is already history, having become so within the past few years. The nation of Israel is in the land today. The sinews and flesh of national organization have bound them together, and now the skin has appeared. Israel is developing her own army and navy, her own political, military and economic defenses and taking her place politically among the nations of the world. All this is recent history.

Only one more thing remains, the spiritual revival of the nation and their recognition by God. Let me add here that the re-establishment of Israel in the land as a nation today is *not* yet the final restoration predicted in the Bible. That will only occur after the coming of their Messiah Christ. When He comes they will receive Him as their King, confess their sin of rejecting Him, and then, after the terrible last great war of this dispensation, the entire remnant of the house of Israel will be returned to their own land, never to depart again. The present rehabilitation in Palestine is only a shadow of the coming restoration, it is only a political and economic move and not the final spiritual awakening.

According to Ezekiel these five things must first happen, and then will follow the last step, the breathing of the Spirit of God into this politically alive but spiritually dead nation, and when that occurs, God will make the restoration complete according to the promises of His sure Word. The remarkable thing is that these first five things, the noise of persecution, the shaking and the moving of the bones together, the organization in the land, the recognition of Israel by the nations, is already fulfilled and the next step is the coming of their King and the final, complete, spiritual as well as national revival of Israel shall take place, and the Lord will reign in

Jerusalem over the house of Jacob forever. How near that day must be we may gather from the fact that the stage is all set for Christ's return. The recent activities among the dry bones are the sure indication of the next step, the coming of Israel's Messiah, to bring in the Kingdom of Heaven upon the earth.

Chapter Three

God's Promise to Israel

Apart from the plain ahd simple plan of salvation, there is no revelation more clear and unmistakable than the revelation concerning the restoration of the nation of Israel to the land of Palestine in the end time, never to leave it again. We have tried to show how the valley of dry bones in Ezekiel thirty-seven clearly predicted this, but it is only one of hundreds of other passages equally clear as to the literal return of Israel as a nation to the land. These prophecies cannot be ignored any longer when we consider that within our own generation, yea within the past few years, we have already seen a partial fulfillment of these predictions. Prophetically, the rebirth of the nation of Israel in the land of Palestine after 2,500 years of dispersion and persecution among the nations ranks as the most significant happening since the coming of Christ 1,900 years ago. It signifies the approach of the end of the age, the consummation of the program begun by God when He first called Israel as a nation out of Egypt and settled them in the land of Canaan.

Most Bible students are familiar with Ezekiel thirty-seven, but many have never carefully studied the preceding chapter which is an introduction and key to the understanding of the vision of the valley of dry bones of Ezekiel thirty-seven. In the thirty-sixth chapter God predicts the restoration of Israel in clear, literal language and then repeats the same truth again in the form of a vision, the valley of dry bones. We need do little more than simply read a few verses in Ezekiel thirty-six to prepare us for Ezekiel thirty-seven.

> Moreover the word of the Lord came unto me, saying,
> Son of man, when the house of Israel dwelt in their own land, they defiled it by their own way and by their own doings: their way was before me as the uncleanness of a removed woman.
> Wherefore I poured my fury upon them for the blood that they had shed upon the land, and for their idols wherewith they had polluted it:
> And I scattered them among the nations, and they were dispersed through the countries according to their way and according to their doings I judged them (Ezekiel 36:16-19).

Surely, little comment is needed here. The language is plain and direct and the testimony of history confirms the truth of these words. The Bible records that when Israel dwelt in their own land they disobeyed God and as a result were cast out of their land and dispersed among all nations and throughout all countries. This is simple history which no one denies. However, that is not the whole story, for God has something more to say:

> Therefore say unto the house of Israel, Thus saith the Lord God; I do not this for your sakes, O house of Israel, but for mine holy name's sake, which ye have profaned among the nations, whither ye went.
> And I will sanctify my great name, which was profaned among the nations, which ye have profaned in the midst of them; and the nations shall know that I am the Lord, saith the Lord God, when I shall be sanctified in you before their eyes.
> For I will take you from among the nations, and gather you out of all countries, and will bring you into your own land.
> And ye shall dwell in the land that I gave to your fathers; and ye shall be my people, and I will be your God.
> And the desolate land shall be tilled, whereas it lay desolate in the sight of all that passed by.

> Then the nations that are left round about you shall
> know that I the Lord build the ruined places, and plant that
> that was desolate: I the Lord have spoken it, and I will do
> it (Ezekiel 36:22-24, 28, 34, 36).

Surely the Holy Spirit could not have made this truth
any plainer and yet, such is the perversity of human
nature that men will read passages like this and yet miss
the truth of Israel's literal restoration entirely. In this
chapter we have two prophecies. First we have the prediction of Israel's dispersion among all nations. This has
been literally fulfilled and is accepted by all Bible students
as a literal prophecy concerning her scattering among
the nations. No other construction can possibly be placed
upon it. In this very same chapter, as it were in the
very same breath, the prophet under the same inspiration
tells us of the re-gathering of this same nation in the
land of their fathers, the restoration of the land of Canaan
and the blessing of the Gentiles when Israel is again in
her own land. To take the first prophecy of the scattering
literally and then to spiritualize the latter prophecy concerning Israel's restorations is to violate every sane prin-
ciple of Bible interpretation and make the Scriptures a
mass of silly contradictions and inconsistencies.

IN PROCESS OF FULFILLMENT

We can the better understand these prophecies today because we are living in the very shadows of their fulfillment. A token and a remnant of Israel is already in the
land and the structure and framework of a national
government has already been formed. However, we believe that the final restoration of Israel permanently in
the land of Canaan will not be the result of man's program but an act of God, which will mean not only their
national restoration but their spiritual revival.

According to the Scriptures, the next event on God's
prophetic program is the coming of Christ *for* the church.
This is the translation of the Body of Christ. When Jesus

comes in the *rapture* or *translation,* He will descend from heaven with a shout, the voice of the archangel and the trump of God (I Thessalonians 4). All the believing dead of all ages will be resurrected, living believers will be changed (I Corinthians 15:51-52) and these will be caught up together to meet the Lord *in the air.* At this coming of Jesus He will not come to the earth, but will shout *from the air* and believers will be caught up to meet the Lord *in the air.* Then, after the church is gone, there will follow a period of seven years of *Tribulation,* also called the *day of the Lord* and the *Time of Jacob's trouble.* During this brief but intense period God will open the seals and pour out the vials of wrath, described in detail in the Book of Revelation. During this period the whole nation of Israel will be re-gathered into Canaan, the temple will be rebuilt, the Old Testament worship and sacrifices re-established, only to have the man of sin, the antichrist, suddenly turn upon them and seek to destroy them from the earth forever. He will gather the armies of the world against Jerusalem and then suddenly, the Lord Jesus, the Messiah, will come from heaven *with his bride,* the Church, and deliver Israel, destroy the armies of antichrist and bind Satan, and then set up His Messianic Kingdom, with its capital in Jerusalem, and there will follow one thousand years of peace upon the earth.

THIS IS GOD'S PROGRAM

Such is the program of Scripture, and all prophecy fits into this framework. Unless one recognizes this program, much of the prophetic Scriptures must of necessity remain utterly unintelligible. Lest you should think this is merely another interpretation of man, note a number of Scriptures which set forth these truths in all clearness. Time would utterly fail us to even quote the hundreds of passages throughout the Scriptures bearing on this point, but we trust that these few will serve as an appetizer to search out this line of truth more carefully for yourself.

Jeremiah, the weeping prophet, has much to say along this line. Here are only a few of his prophecies:

> Therefore, hehold, the days come, saith the Lord, that it shall no more be said, The Lord liveth, that brought up the children of Israel out of the land of Egypt;
>
> But, The Lord liveth, that brought up the children of Israel from the land of the north, and from all lands whither he had driven them: and I will bring them again into their land that I gave unto their fathers.
>
> Behold, I will send for many fishers, saith the Lord, and they shall fish them; and after will I send for many hunters, and they shall hunt them from every mountain, and from every hill, and out of the holes of the rocks (Jeremiah 16: 14-16).

In the same vein the prophet tells us a few more details in the twenty-third chapter:

> And I will gather the remnant of my flock out of all countries whither I have driven them, and will bring them again to their folds; and they shall be fruitful and increase.
>
> Behold, the days come, saith the Lord, that I will raise unto David a righteous Branch, and a King shall reign and prosper, and shall execute judgment and justice in the earth.
>
> In his days Judah shall be saved, and Israel shall dwell safely: and this is his name whereby he shall be called, The Lord Our Righteousness (Jeremiah 23:3, 5, 6).

HE WILL JUDGE THE NATIONS

When the Lord sets His hand to re-gather all of Israel into the land again, He then too will deal with the nations which have persecuted her. At the close of the tribulation, the time of Jacob's Trouble, the Lord will punish and reward all nations on the basis of their dealings and treatment of the nation of Israel. God's promise to Abraham, "I will bless them that bless thee, and curse him that curseth thee," will then be fulfilled.

> But fear not thou, O my servant Jacob, and be not dismayed, O Israel: for, behold, I will save thee from afar off, and thy seed from the land of their captivity; and Jacob shall return, and be in rest and at ease, and none shall make him afraid.

> Fear thou not, O Jacob my servant, saith the Lord: for I am with thee; for I will make a full end of all the nations whither I have driven thee: but I will not make a full end of thee, but correct thee in measure; yet will I not leave thee wholly unpunished.

Passage after passage might be quoted which deal with God's promises to the house of Israel. During this present church age the nation is temporarily set aside while the Church is being called out, and as soon as that occurs, and we may look for it any time, God will set His hand to fulfill all these promises and to establish Israel forever in the land. This has never yet occured in all history. Each time Israel has been driven away from the land again, but the time will soon be here when they shall return never to leave it. Amos the prophet tells of this in glowing and unmistakable terms:

> And I will bring again the captivity of my people of Israel, and they shall build the waste cities, and inhabit them; and they shall plant vineyards, and drink the wine thereof, they shall also make gardens, and eat the fruit of them.
> And I will plant them upon their land, and they shall no more be pulled up out of their land which I have given them, saith the Lord thy God (Amos 9:14-15).

Since this has never yet been fulfilled, it still lies in the future and from all indications, the very near future. "Even so, come, Lord Jesus."

Chapter Four

The Lost Ten Tribes

> The word of the Lord came again unto me, saying,
> Moreover, thou son of man, take thee one stick, and
> write upon it, For Judah, and for the children of Israel
> his companions: then take another stick, and write upon it,
> For Joseph, the stick of Ephraim, and for all the house of
> Israel his companions:
> And join them one to another into one stick; and they
> shall become one in thine hand (Ezekiel 37:15-17).

THIS SIGN OF THE TWO STICKS in the hands of the
prophet Ezekiel is a continuation of the vision of the
valley of dry bones in the preceding part of this chapter.
The valley of dry bones which Ezekiel saw was the whole
house of Israel, scattered today among the nations, but
one day to be revived and settled again into their own
land. This sign of the two sticks deals with the same subject, only adding some very important details, already suggested in the vision of the dry bones. The prophet is to
take two sticks and write on one stick the name Judah,
and upon the other stick the name Israel. Then he is to
bring the two together and they shall become one stick
in his hand.

As in the case of the valley of dry bones, we are not
left in doubt as to the meaning of this sign, but as usual
the key hangs right by the door and the Lord Himself
gives us the meaning of this strange sign. Here is God's
own interpretation:

And when the children of thy people shall speak unto thee, saying, Wilt thou not shew us what thou meanest by these?

Say unto them, Thus saith the Lord God; Behold, I will take the stick of Joseph, which is in the hand of Ephraim, and the tribes of Israel his fellows, and will put them with him, even with the stick of Judah, and make them one stick, and they shall be one in mine hand.

And the sticks whereon thou writest shall be in thine hand before their eyes.

And say unto them, Thus saith the Lord God; Behold, I will take the children of Israel from among the nations, whither they be gone, and will gather them on every side, and bring them into their own land:

And I will make them one nation in the land upon the mountains of Israel; and one king shall be king to them all: and they shall be no more two nations, neither shall they be divided into two kingdoms any more at all (Ezekiel 37:18-22).

THE TWELVE TRIBES DIVIDE

The meaning is perfectly clear. The day is coming, says the prophet, when the Twelve Tribes of Israel who were together under David and King Solomon shall be re-gathered in the land and made to be one single kingdom again. To understand the meaning of these words we must for a moment review Israel's history.

After King Solomon died, his son, Rehoboam, became king over Israel. The people, burdened under the heavy taxation of Solomon's reign, requested of the new king Rehoboam that the burden be lifted. But Rehoboam listened to his young counselors instead of the older leaders of Israel, and instead of granting the request of the people promised them even a heavier yoke and still more burdensome taxes. As a result of this, an insurrection and rebellion resulted and the northern ten tribes of Israel seceded from the southern two tribes. They chose Jeroboam to be their king while Rehoboam remained king over the southern kingdom. A continual war resulted between these two kingdoms, the southern kingdom consisting of the two tribes, Judah and Benjamin, and the northern kingdom composed of the remaining ten tribes of the sons of Jacob. The southern kingdom became known as Judah and the northern became known as Israel. So there were two opposing kingdoms, Judah and Israel.

THE FINAL CAPTIVITY

After about 150 years of this division into two kingdoms, the Assyrians descended upon the northern kingdom and defeated it, carrying the Israelites captive into Assyria from whence they were scattered throughout the world and have never returned to this day. Then some eighty years later the king of Babylon, Nebuchadnezzar, besieged the city of Jerusalem, and carried the southern kingdom of Judah into Babylon as captives. While the captives from the ten tribes of the northern kingdom never returned in any great number but remained scattered among the nations, the captives of Judah did return in part, seventy years later.

Under Zerubbabel, Nehemiah and Ezra some forty thousand members of the kingdom of Judah returned to the land of Palestine and were there at the time Jesus was born in Bethlehem. These members of the southern kingdom came to be known as Jews, from the word Judah. The Jews of Jesus' day were largely this remnant from the restored tribes of Judah and Benjamin. The Jews of today also are the scattered descendants of this body of Judah. About Seventy A. D. these Jews were again thrust out of the land by the Romans, and under Titus the city of Jerusalem was destroyed and the Jews scattered throughout the nations where the ten tribes had already been for over six hundred years.

WHERE ARE THE TEN TRIBES?

Now, according to Ezekiel, who himself was a captive in Babylon, the northern ten tribes (Israel) and the southern two tribes (Judah) represented by the Jews of today are to be brought together and reunited once more in the land of Palestine. There has been a great deal of conjecture as to who the lost ten tribes are, and where they are today. There are those who claim that the Anglo-Saxon peoples are the true Israel. Others say that the Ethiopians are the ten tribes. All are agreed about the Jews as representing Judah, but with Israel it is different. There are several religious sects who claim that they are the 144,000, while others who indulge in the spiritualizing of Scripture and prophecy claim that the Church is spiritual Israel and God is all through with both the Jews and Israel as far as their return to the land and their establishment in the kingdom is concerned. To accept this view, however, necessitates the throwing away of this entire thirty-seventh chapter of Ezekiel and many other parts of the Scriptures.

To state dogmatically *who* the lost ten tribes are is perhaps impossible. Frankly, we must admit that we do not know. It is enough that *God* knows where they are and that is what counts. When the time comes for this regathering the Lord will not overlook a single one, for He himself says:

> And it shall come to pass in that day, that the Lord shall set his hand again the second time to recover the remnant of his people, which shall be left, from Assyria, and from Egypt, and from Pathros, and from Cush, and from Elam, and from Shinar, and from Hamath, and from the islands of the sea.
>
> And he shall set up an ensign for the nations, and shall assemble the outcasts of Israel, and gather together the dispersed of Judah from the four corners of the earth (Isaiah 11:11-12).
>
> And it shall come to pass in that day, that the Lord shall beat off from the channel of the river unto the stream of Egypt, and ye shall be gathered one by one, O ye children of Israel (Isaiah 27:12).

THE HUNDRED FORTY-FOUR THOUSAND

John in Revelation 7 and 14 tells us of this restoration of the 144,000 from the *twelve* Tribes of Israel, and enumerates the Twelve Tribes from which they will come, dropping Dan because out of it will come the antichrist, and substituting another in its place. Again we remind you that there are many signs indicating that this movement is already begun. The political establishment of the nation of Israel in the land is the first step. The stick of Judah is already in Palestine, according to God's order by which he will save the tents of Judah first. Judah will first be re-gathered and then will follow the other ten tribes.

How Near is the Restoration

Since the movement is already begun, we can imagine how near we must be to the final restoration of *all* Israel to the land. But before the nation is fully restored to the land, the Lord Jesus *must first return* to take out the Church, the Body of Christ. Israel will not be spiritually resurrected till after the Rapture. Before that glorious day for Israel dawns, David the king must first come back, for in the kingdom age, David will be their king in Jerusalem. Christ shall be King over all the earth with the church reigning with Him as the bride, and David will be the king of Israel under King Jesus. This being true, the resurrection must first take place and this we know will occur at the coming of Christ for His Church.

Ezekiel leaves no doubt about this, but tells us:

> And David my servant shall be king over them; (over the united kingdom of Judah and Israel) and they all shall have one shepherd . . .
> And they shall dwell in the land that I have given unto Jacob my servant, wherein your fathers have dwelt; and they shall dwell therein, even they, and their children, and their children's children for ever: and my servant David shall be their prince for ever (Ezekiel 37:24-25).

This then necessitates a resurrection first. When Ezekiel wrote these words David had long been dead and buried. Yet the Word of God says that when Israel is established in the land David shall be their king and their prince forever. There is only one answer and that answer is the

First Resurrection. Before the kingdom is set up, the Lord will come to raise the dead and snatch His church away, to return seven years later to set up the Kingdom with David the king, and the twelve apostles sitting on twelve thrones judging the Twelve Tribes of Israel. In I Thessalonians 4 we have the record of this glorious event of the Resurrection when

> the Lord himself shall descend from heaven with a shout, with the voice of the archangel, and with the trump of God: and the dead in Christ shall rise first:
>
> Then we which are alive and remain shall be caught up together with them in clouds, to meet the Lord in the air: and so shall we ever be with the Lord (I Thessalonians 4:16-17).

How wonderful God's Word, how harmonious its revelation. How simple to understand, how easy to interpret, if we simply read it as God gave it, and not try to put our own interpretation upon it or seek to twist God's Word by spiritualizing it to conform to our prejudices and tradition.

To sum up the sign of the two sticks, then, we have this wonderful revelation. God knows where all the Twelve Tribes of Israel are. He will re-gather them for the setting up of the Kingdom of the Messiah for one thousand blessed years. Before this occurs, Jesus must first return to raise the believing dead of all ages, take His Church to heaven, then to return *with* the Church to set up the kingdom. In the interval between the first resurrection and the coming of Christ to set up the kingdom will be the time of Jacob's Trouble, when Israel shall pass through the fire, the dry bones shall be made alive and gathered in the land, converted as a nation to faith in their Messiah, Jesus Christ, and enjoy the blessing of the Lord forever.

Since we sincerely believe that the present world events, the formation of the northern confederacy, and the pacts binding the old Roman Empire territory together, the atomic bomb, the cold war, earthquakes and all the other signs definitely herald the coming of Christ to set up the

kingdom, and the Rapture must take place seven years before this, we would ask, *How near must the coming of the
Lord be?* What a glorious hope for the believer; what a
terrible thing for the unsaved, when the door of mercy
closes and the day of grace ends forever for those who
have rejected the free offer of salvation through faith in
Jesus Christ.

> He which testifieth these things saith, Surely, I come
> quickly. Amen. Even so, come, Lord Jesus (Revelation
> 22:20).

Chapter Five

THE ABRAHAMIC COVENANT

A discussion of the dry bones of Ezekiel 37 would hardly be complete without at least a little more attention to the subject at Palestine as it relates to the future setting up of the kingdom of the Lord Jesus Christ. This becomes all the more important when we realize that Palestine has been so much in the news and the activity in the land of Canaan promised to Abraham and his seed is the subject of the greatest controversy before the nations. The history of this land begins way back in the book of Genesis, when God spoke to Abraham and gave him the covenant which included possession of the land as well as the possession of the land by his physical seed which God promised to him at that time.

> And when Abram was ninety years old and nine, the Lord appeared to Abram, and said unto him, I am the Almighty God; walk before me, and be thou perfect.
> And I will make my covenant between me and thee, and will multiply thee exceedingly.
> And I will establish my covenant between me and thee and thy seed after thee in their generations for an everlasting covenant, to be a God unto thee, and to thy seed after thee.
> And I will give unto thee, and to thy seed after thee, the land wherein thou art a stranger, all the land of Canaan, for an everlasting possession; and I will be their God (Genesis 17:1, 2, 7, 8).

No country in all the world has been so much in the news and in the public eye in recent years as the land of Palestine, also called the Land of Israel, the Land of Promise, the Land of Canaan and the Glorious Land. Not only is this true, but Palestine has been more important in the entire history of man and the nations than any other land. The whole Bible centers about this country, and the people so closely associated with it, the nation of Israel.

However, her history has only begun. Palestine is the land of history, to be sure, but it is predominately the land of the future, the land of prophecy. While much of the Bible is a history of the nation of Israel in the land of Palestine, the prophetic books of Scripture are concerned almost exclusively with the Palestine of the future and the future of its people, Israel.

THE GEOGRAPHICAL CENTER OF THE WORLD

In Scripture, Palestine is the exact geographic center of the world's surface. By this we mean that directions in the Bible are always with reference to and in relation to Palestine. North in Scripture always means north of Palestine. South means south of Palestine, and so too, with east and with west.

In the very same way Palestine in Scripture is the historical center of the world. Bible history and geography deal with the land of Canaan, its people, and its future. Other lands are only mentioned in Scripture because they have had some contact, some dealing or relationship with this one land. Nations which have no connection with Palestine are never mentioned.

Moreover, Palestine is the religious center of the entire world. In the region just north of Palestine man began his existence in the garden of Eden, in the cradle of the human race, in the general region of the Euphrates River. Here God called Abraham. Here God gave His laws in the region of Sinai, part of the original grant of Canaan which God gave to Abraham. Here God chose to send His Son to be born of a Virgin in Palestine. Here the Son of

God spent His entire ministry, in Palestine. He never left its frontiers, except once when as a child He and His parents were compelled to flee into Egypt.

Here Christ taught, suffered, died, rose and ascended into heaven, and here it is that He will come again. When He returns it will not be to the United States or to Britain or to Rome, but to the land of Palestine. Jerusalem, its capital, is the eternal city, not the city of Rome. All others will be destroyed, but Jerusalem shall be a praise forever unto the Lord.

All these things about Palestine have been mentioned that you may know what great importance God places on this land of Canaan, and this importance is borne out by secular history as well. Palestine has been, and still is, the prize country of the entire world. More battles have been fought over, more blood has been shed in, more expensive and gory campaigns have been waged for, the possession of Palestine than any other country of the world in all of its battle-filled history.

PALISTINE TODAY

Today, Palestine is the powder keg of the nations. It is truly dynamite, sputtering and fizzling and threatening to explode at any moment. The biggest headache Britain has ever had is Palestine. A more vexing problem than India or Egypt was the problem of the land of Canaan, and we shall attempt to show in these chapters that the turbulent history of England and her recent trials and tribulations have a very direct relation to her connection with the land and her dealing with the land of Palestine. Britain is frantically seeking to interest even the United States to join with her in an attempt to solve the apparently insoluble problem of the land, the Holy Land.

WHY ALL THE COMMOTION?

We are led to ask, therefore, why all of this disturbance over Palestine? When we consider its size and its apparent unimportance, and the fact that Palestine is only a little strip of territory about one-hundred-and-fifty miles long, from twenty to sixty miles in breadth, lying between Dan to the north and bounded by Beersheba in the south, and limited by the Jordan Valley to the east and the Mediterranean Sea to the west we wonder why all the disturbance. Palestine contains less than six thousand square miles, and much of this area is a desert waste, especially about the Dead Sea in the south. The balance, a considerable amount of it, at least, is untillable mountains. Yet the productive part of this land was once the most fruitful in all the world, and although comparatively waste and unproductive today, as for many centuries past, it is now being developed in a way unprecedented in all of history. The land contains greater wealth per square foot than any other country still waiting to be developed.

God called it a land of corn and wine, a land of milk and of honey, and prophecy tells us that when Israel shall again be restored to the land of Canaan in the millennial age, it will rival the garden of Eden for beauty and for fruitfulness.

PALESTINE AND CANAAN

Before giving more facts concerning the land called the Holy Land and the Glorious Land and the Promised Land, we must point out something very important which is almost entirely overlooked by most Bible students. Palestine and Canaan are not synonymous terms. The name Palestine is not the real Scriptural name for the promised land which God gave by covenant to Abraham and his seed. The name which God gives to the land which He promised to Abraham is "the land of Canaan," a great tract of country extending from the river Nile in Egypt to the Mediterranean Sea in the west, and reaching north to the country of Iran and the Euphrates River. That is Scripturally the land of Canaan. Its boundaries are defined in Genesis 15:18-21:

In the same day the Lord made a covenant with Abram, saying, Unto thy seed have I given this land, from the river of Egypt unto the great river, the river Euphrates:
The Kenites, and the Kenizzites, and the Kadmonites,
And the Hittites, and the Perizzites, and the Rephaims,
And the Amorites, and the Canaanites, and the Girgashites, and the Jebusites.

From this you will notice that God promised a tract of land many, many times larger than present-day Palestine. Please bear that distinction in mind. Palestine is that small part of the land of Canaan situated west of the Jordan River. It is included as a part of the land of Canaan but is not technically the land of Canaan. The word Palestine, oddly enough, occurs only four times in the entire Bible. It is referred to in Exodus 15:14, then again twice in Isaiah fourteen, and once in Joel three. In each one of these references the reference is not to Israel, but to the heathen nations which occupied that part that we know today as the land of Palestine. The word Palestine itself comes from the word Philistines, who were the occupants of this strip of land when Israel came to take over possession of the land of Canaan.

THE LAND OF CANAAN

So Canaan is the promised land, and Palestine is only a part of that promised land. Because Israel never possessed all of the land of Canaan, but only that portion known to us as Palestine, the name Palestine is applied to the Holy Land as though it included all of the grant that God gave to Abraham. We want it made clear that this is not the correct interpretation of Scripture. However, we shall, because of the common usage of the name Palestine, use it as also referring to the Promised land of Israel, remembering all the time that God's original grant included the whole of Canaan from Egypt to the Euphrates River.

Canaan was a grandson of Noah. In Genesis 9:20-26 we have the record of Ham who was the father of Canaan.

Because of the sin of Ham during his father Noah's drunkenness, Noah pronounced a curse upon his grandson Canaan. When the people of the world thereafter spread out upon the earth, the descendants of this Canaan, grandson of Noah, moved into the region of Palestine and settled there, and became the Canaanites, and the tribes which were found there when Abraham was called from Ur of the Chaldees. Hence the name, the land of Canaan, means primarily the country where the Canaanites, the descendants of the grandson of Noah, had settled and were dwelling.

THE CALL OF ABRAHAM

About 2,500 years before Christ, God called a man by the name of Abram, who was a Gentile, an idol worshipper in the Ur of the Chaldees, the site of ancient Babylon, and made with him a covenant of grace, an everlasting covenant. In this unbreakable, everlasting covenant, God promised to the seed of Abraham, through Isaac and through Jacob and his twelve sons, the nation of Israel, (including the people we know today as the Jews) the entire land of Canaan as their possession forever. In history this nation Israel, the Twelve Tribes of Jacob, possessed only a fraction of this promised land, but in prophecy God tells us they will at some future time, in the near future we believe, possess and inhabit all of it, never to be driven out again.

Recognition of this fact is the solution to the problem of Palestine. Until the nations recognize this ancient covenant God made with Abraham and search the Scriptures for the answer to the Palestinian question, the solution to Palestine will never be found. The Bible is the most ancient document in existence which deals with the problem of Palestine, the problem which vexes the nations today. How foolish, therefore, that in seeking to solve this puzzle, men will not turn to the only authentic and the most ancient of all the records concerning this land.

We shall study this covenant which God made with Abraham, and which four thousand years afterwards is still as binding and unbreakable as in the day when it was given. It is still in effect, though it has been postponed now for all these many, many years. Before you read the next chapter of this book, you should study carefully Genesis 12, 13, 15 and 17 which give us the first record of the covenant which God gave to Abraham by an everlasting promise, by an oath, wherein God cannot lie.

Before we close this chapter however, we want to view the practical conclusion. A covenant of grace can never be broken, as we shall point out abundantly when we study in the next chapter the covenant God made with Abraham. The covenant God made concerning the land of Palestine and Israel is still in effect. Even though the nation may be suffering because of its disobedience, ultimately God is going to fulfill every condition of that covenant which He promised, and that is true today. God has never changed. Once an individual is in the covenant of God's grace, he is in it forever. Disobedience and sin may bring upon the individual God's chastening, even as Israel as a nation today is scattered and persecuted and is paying for her sin, but ultimately God will keep His promise in every detail. The God of Israel has never changed. He said, "I am the Lord, I change not." It is His unbreakable promise. And so, if you will receive Christ as your personal Saviour, you will be a member of the body of Christ, included in the covenant of God's grace forever. If you disobey, God will chasten you, but once He says, "Thou art mine," there is no breaking of His Word.

Chapter Six

THE RETURN OF ISRAEL

> And I will establish my covenant between me and thee
> and thy seed after thee in their generations for an everlasting
> covenant, to be a God unto thee, and to thy seed after thee.
>   And I will give unto thee, and to thy seed after thee,
> the land wherein thou art a stranger, all the land of Canaan,
> for an everlasting possession; and I will be their God
> (Genesis 17:7, 8).

IN A PREVIOUS CHAPTER we gave a number of interesting
and important facts about the land of Palestine, the Holy
Land, the land God promised to the descendants of Jacob,
the Twelve Tribes of Israel, for an everlasting possession.
Now we shall study the covenant of Abraham in greater
detail, and find that it holds the solution to the vexing
perennial problem of Palestine. Just recently the land
was bathed in human blood and torn by strife, hatred and
dissension between Arab and Jew, while Britain tore her
hair in anguish in seeking a solution for the problem. The
entire answer would immediately be found if the leaders
of our nations and our diplomats would only study what
the Bible has to say concerning this problem and turn
to the Word of God and follow its instructions.

ABRAHAM AND CANAAN

Twenty-five hundred years before Christ, God called
a man named Abraham to leave his home in Chaldea and
go to a new and strange land. In this call of Abraham,
God began a new thing in the history of humanity. After

42

the flood God had in a measure left man to himself, but man soon proved the incorrigibility of his own heart and promptly forgot God. The knowledge of Jehovah all but passed from the earth. Therefore, God gave up the nations and called a single man by the name of Abram to become the father of a new nation of a predestinated, foreordained, elected people, the nation of Israel. In order to prevent the knowledge of God from disappearing completely from the earth, He ordained that through this nation He would give His revelation, preserve the true religion of Jehovah, and out of Abraham's line bring forth the Redeemer of Israel and of the world.

THE CALL OF ABRAHAM

In Genesis 12 we are told of the call of this man and the first mention of God's covenant with him. In Genesis 11 we have the record of man's utter failure after the flood, and the story of how God called Abram out of the Ur of the Chaldees to go into the land of Canaan is told in Chapter 12.

> Now the Lord had said unto Abram, Get thee out of thy country, and from thy kindred, and from thy father's house, unto a land that I will shew thee:
>
> And I will make of thee a great nation, and I will bless thee, and make thy name great; and thou shalt be a blessing:
>
> And I will bless them that bless thee, and curse him that curseth thee; and in thee shall all families of the earth be blessed (Genesis 12:1-3).

This is the first statement of the covenant which God made with Abraham. Notice here the two elements of this covenant, and do not miss them. First, this covenant had to do with a specific *land* called the land of Canaan. Second, it has to do with a physical *seed,* the descendants of Abraham through Isaac, Jacob and the Twelve Tribes of Israel. If those two thoughts are borne in mind, the Bible will become perfectly clear in the matter of God's program for Israel and the land. The *land* is Palestine. The *seed* refers to the Twelve Tribes of Israel.

Then a third element is introduced. God promises to preserve both the land and the people forever and ever. He promises a blessing on those who show favor to the seed, Israel, and the land, but prophesies a curse upon those who will persecute His people or confiscate the land which God called, "My land." Here are the words of God again, in Genesis 12:3: "And I will bless them that bless thee, and curse him that curseth thee."

In the next chapter, Genesis 13, this covenant which God introduces in Genesis 12 is confirmed, and in verses 14 to 16 we read God's Word as follows:

> And the Lord said unto Abram, after that Lot was separated from him, Lift up now thine eyes, and look from the place where thou art northward, and southward, and eastward, and westward:
>
> For all the land which thou seest, to thee will I give it, and to thy seed for ever.
>
> And I will make thy seed as the dust of the earth: so that if a man can number the dust of the earth, then shall thy seed also be numbered.

Notice the two things which stand out in this passage. God speaks of a *land,* a literal land which Abraham was able to see with his physical eye, and then He speaks to him of a *seed.* Again we repeat, the land is Palestine, the people are Israel, Abraham's seed through Isaac and Jacob. Never think of Palestine without Israel. Never think of Israel without Palestine. When they are united the world is at peace. When they are separated, the people and the land apart, the world is in turmoil, confusion and convulsion.

SEVEN STATEMENTS OF THE COVENANT

In all, God gave the promise of the seed and the land to Abraham no less then seven times in order to emphasize the absolute certainty of His Word. In Genesis 15 God appears once more to Abraham after his reassertion of faith in Jehovah, and says in verse 18:

> In the same day the Lord made a covenant with Abram,

saying, Unto thy seed have I given this land, from the river of Egypt unto the great river, the river Euphrates.

In this repetition of the covenant God adds some more details. First notice, God says, "Unto thy seed have I given this land." You will notice the past tense is used here. In Genesis 12 and 13 God had said, "Will I give it" but in chapter 15 He says, "Unto thy seed *have* I given this land." Abraham had no seed as yet. He was still childless and advancing in years, and still God says, "Unto thy seed have I given this land." As far as God was concerned it was already done. This form of expression, frequently found in Scripture where God speaks of future things as though they had already transpired, is called a "Prophetic Perfect". Although it still lies in the future, with God it was as good as done. In the mind of the Almighty it was already accomplished, for God has no past, God has no future, but lives in the eternal present. He revealed Himself later to Moses as the "I am that I am," in the present tense, you will notice. He does not say, "I was that I was" or "I will be that I will be" but emphatically He says, "I am." With God all things are in the present, for God cannot change.

In the very same way, we, the children of God today, are said to have been chosen in Him from the foundation of the world, and Christ is said to be the Lamb slain from before the foundation of the world. When God promises, it is as good as done. There is never any question as to whether He will keep His Word.

Secondly, notice that God gives in Genesis 15:18 the boundaries of the land which He is going to give to Abraham's seed. They are as follows: "From the river of Egypt (Nile) unto the great river, the river Euphrates."

This gigantic tract of land Israel has never yet possessed and therefore its possessions must still lie in the future since God always keeps His Word. It is a tract of land over five hundred miles square containing between two-hundred-and-fifty and three-hundred-thousand square miles, some fifty times greater than the land of Palestine as we speak of it today. To identify this land so there may be no mistake as to what God refers, He enumerates the nations which are at that particular time occupying the land.

> The Kenites, and the Kenizzites, and the Kadmonites,
> And the Hittites, and the Perizzites, and the Rephaims,
> And the Amorites, and the Canaanites, and the Girgashites,
> and the Jebusites (Genesis 15:19-21).

This detail is given in order that there may be no question but that God is referring to the literal land of Canaan then inhabited by these literal tribes.

In Genesis, chapter 17, God repeats to Abraham the covenant, the passage given at the beginning of this chapter, and you will remember that here God gives to Abraham the term during which He will give the land of Canaan to Abraham's seed. It is to be forever. God says "For an everlasting possession." In verse seven He says: "And I will establish my covenant between me and thee and thy seed after thee in their generations, for an everlasting covenant" (Genesis 17:7).

In the eighth verse He says: ". . . all the land of Canaan, for an everlasting posession" (Genesis 17:8).

Here lies the very key, then, to the problem of Palestine. According to the Word of God it belongs to Israel by an everlasting covenant which can never be annulled or broken or set aside.

THE SECONDARY COVENANT GIVEN

Remember, therefore, that the promise of God to Abraham was a covenant of grace, unconditional, absolute and eternal. Canaan today is still the heritage of the Twelve Tribes of Israel even though it may be in the hands of another people or nations. Four hundred and thirty years after God made this promise to Abraham, after Abraham himself was dead and the promised seed had just been delivered from the land of Egypt, God through Moses upon Mount Sinai made a secondary covenant with the nation. This was the covenant of law, a covenant of works, a conditional agreement whose blessing depended on Israel's behavior, conduct and works and obedience and not alone upon God's faithfulness.

In this covenant of works God promised to Israel certain blessings in the promised land upon the condition of obedience. If they would be disobedient and break this law, it would mean chastening, tribulation and sorrow, and they would be driven out, scattered from the Promised Land among all the nations of the world. Here are the words of God as found in Deuteronomy 28:15-19:

> But it shall come to pass, if thou wilt not hearken unto the voice of the Lord thy God, to observe to do all his commandments and his statues which I command thee this day; that all these curses shall come upon thee, and overtake thee:
>
> Cursed shalt thou be in the city, and cursed shalt thou be in the field.
>
> Cursed shall be thy basket and thy store.
>
> Cursed shall be the fruit of thy body, and the fruit of thy land, the increase of thy kine, and the flocks of thy sheep.
>
> Cursed shalt thou be when thou comest in, and cursed shalt thou be when thou goest out.

In verse sixty-four we hear God saying:

> And the Lord shall scatter thee among all people, from the one end of the earth even unto the other; and there thou shalt serve other gods, which neither thou nor thy fathers have known, even wood and stone.

Certainly comment is unnecessary when we remember how literally these words have been fulfilled in the history of God's scattered people.

GRACE STILL STANDS

The following is the most important fact in regard to God's dealings with the nation. Most people think that God is all through with Israel and the Jews because they have failed under this covenant of the Law. They forget that the covenant of Abraham, the covenant of grace, antedated by four hundred and thirty years the covenant of works and even anticipated Israel's failure. The covenant of grace is, therefore, unaffected by the covenant of works.

The original promise of Palestine as the ultimate and everlasting possession of the Twelve Tribes still stands even though Israel has sinned, broken God's law and is suffering many, many centuries for their sin. God will yet remember His unconditional covenant of grace to Abraham, Isaac and Jacob. Listen, therefore, to God's promise after He has given the list of curses that shall come upon them for their disobedience. Here is the record in Isaiah 14:1-3:

> For the Lord will have mercy on Jacob, and will yet choose Israel, and set them in their own land: and the strangers shall be joined with them, and they shall cleave to the house of Jacob.
> And the people shall take them, and bring them to their place: and the house of Israel shall possess them in the land of the Lord for servants and handmaids: and they shall take them captives, whose captives they were; and they shall rule over their oppressors.
> And it shall come to pass in the day that the Lord shall give thee rest from thy sorrow, and from thy fear, and from the hard bondage wherein thou wast made to serve. . .

Yes, indeed, God will fulfill His promise in spite of His people's unfaithfulness. He will punish them, to be sure, for their sins, but He will not break His covenant with them. In spite of their unworthiness, God's grace will still prevail. One more passage will illustrate this, Hosea 3:4 and 5:

> For the children of Israel shall abide many days without a king, and without a prince, and without a sacrifice, and without an image, and without an ephod, and without teraphim:
> Afterward shall the children of Israel return, and seek the Lord their God, and David their king; and shall fear the Lord and his goodness in the latter days.

I do trust that we will not only see God's faithfulness to the nation of Israel as a covenant-keeping God, but apply the practical application to our own hearts. We ask the question, "Can we trust God?" "Does God keep His Word?" Yes, indeed, God keeps every promise. What a practical lesson all of this holds for us, too. If you have believed on His Son, the Lord Jesus Christ, and have been saved and through faith have appropriated the finished work of Christ to your heart, then you are in God's covenant of grace forever. He says:

> Verily, verily, I say unto you, He that heareth my word, and believeth on him that sent me, hath everlasting life, and shall not come into condemnation; but is passed from death unto life (John 5:24).

There you have it; God will never go back on His promise nor on His Word.

It is also true that if you are disobedient and depart from Him and rebel, you will be chastened. God will deal with you as He did with Israel, but He will not forsake His covenant and His promise. He, who said, "Verily, verily, I say unto you, He that heareth my word, and believeth on him that sent me, hath everlasting life" will never go back on His promise. That still holds, and will hold forever. You may be chastened and suffer for your sin; you may lose your rewards at the Judgment Seat of Christ, but your eternal life is sure, because God, who cannot lie, has said, "By grace are ye saved through faith; and that not of yourselves, it is the gift of God: Not of works, lest any man should boast." God grants us eternal life as a free, unconditional gift based on the satisfactory finished work of the Lord Jesus Christ on Calvary. Dare you trust Him? Trust Him not only to save you but to keep you unto the end, for He that hath begun a good work in us shall consummate and finish and complete it even unto the day of Jesus Christ.

Chapter Seven

THE TWO COVENANTS

> And this I say, that the covenant, that was confirmed before of God in Christ, the law, which was four hundred and thirty years after, cannot disannul, that it should make the promise of none effect.
>
> For if the inheritance be of the law, it is no more of promise: but God gave it to Abraham by promise (Galatians 3:17-18).

GOD MADE A COVENANT OF GRACE with Abraham over two thousand years before the coming of Christ. This covenant was all of grace; that is, God did everything. It was an unconditional covenant and depended solely and entirely upon God's promise and ability to keep His Word. This covenant promised to the nation of Israel, the seed of Abraham, (still unborn) the land of Canaan for an everlasting possession, and it is still in effect and as true now as it was when God gave it.

THE LAW

Four hundred and thirty years after God made His covenant with Abraham, He added another covenant at Mount Sinai which was a covenant of works. Please notice that this secondary covenant was *added*. It did not set aside the first covenant, nor did it supplant the covenant of grace. It had nothing to do with the carrying out of God's covenant to Abraham which preceded it by four hundred and thirty years. It had to do only with the enjoyment or loss of the blessings dependent on their obedience. Of course, we know that they failed under the covenant of the law, and the result was that God came to chasten them and scatter them throughout the entire world.

Here Christians get off the track most frequently. They misunderstand the Abrahamic covenant of grace. They imagine that because Israel failed under the Sinaitic covenant of the law, as everyone else fails under the law, that it means the end of God's national dealings with the nation of Israel. Therefore, they seek to spiritualize God's covenant and forget its primary interpretation to Israel and begin to apply it exclusively to the church of this dispensation. So these spiritualizers argue this way. The Old Testament was typical. Since Calvary, the covenant of Abraham applies to the church, and not to Israel. God is all done with the literal nation of Israel, and they will never go back to possess the promised land of Palestine. The promised land, to them, becomes heaven. Israel becomes the church, and poor Israel is left with a hollow promise which God entirely failed to keep.

If there is any question as to the correctness of these foregoing statements, study very carefully Galatians 3:17 with which this present chapter is begun. Notice carefully what Paul says under inspiration in this passage. He is setting forth the truth of grace, proving that when we are saved by grace it is forever, never to be lost or to be broken. While our disobedience *after* we are saved brings upon us God's displeasure and God's chastening, to be sure, and may mean the loss of rewards at the judgment seat of Christ, it does not in any way affect our eternal life and salvation which is God's free gift, independent of our own works and unconditionally given.

In order to illustrate this fact, and clinch it, Paul uses the covenant of grace to Abraham and the covenant of works at Sinai and says:

And this I say, that the covenant, that was confirmed before of God in Christ, the law, which was four hundred and thirty years after, cannot disannul, that it should make the promise of none effect (Galatians 3:17).

Do not hurry over that passage. It is all-important. Paul says this. Although Israel failed under the law and came under the judgment of God because of its sin, He does not set aside or annul that unconditional covenant of grace which He made four hundred and thirty years earlier. After God has purified and chastened the nation, He will restore it again to the land of Canaan, never to be plucked up. Now, says Paul, so also God deals in grace with us. If He keeps His promise to Israel, in spite of its failure, He will also keep His promise to you who have trusted in Him in spite of all your failures.

If God fails to keep His Word to Abraham, then how do we know that He will keep His promise to us, "That whosoever shall call on the name of the Lord shall be saved," and the promise that "He that heareth my Word and believeth on Him that sent me hath everlasting life . . ."? If God lied to Abraham, He may be lying to us. The question of whether Palestine still belongs to Israel and whether they will ultimately return to possess it forever is far more important than it appears on the surface. The implications are of tremendous importance to every believer. If you are one of those who does not believe that God will literally restore Israel to the land according to His clear promise, then you cannot be sure either of your own salvation, which also depends upon God's simple promise. You have nothing but His Word as your assurance, and if He failed and was unable to keep His promise to Abraham, and his seed in which He said, "I will give unto thee, and to thy seed after thee, the land wherein thou art a stranger, even all the land of Canaan" then how do you know that He will keep His promise, "But as many as received him, to them gave he power to become the sons of God, even to them that believe on his Name"?

God's unconditional promise of grace cannot be destroyed by man's failure or disobedience. So Israel today is scattered among the nations of the world, and for centuries Palestine has been very far from being the land of corn and wine, the land of milk and honey. Instead it has been the land of thorns and thistles for many centuries until just recently in fulfillment of God's Word it is being reclaimed in preparation for Israel's return according to the sure promises of God.

PALISTINE TODAY

Until a few years ago Palestine was largely a waste land. Travellers who went to Palestine came back disillusioned and disappointed. Many have said that it was worthwhile because of the sentiment and history of the land as the place where Christ was born, taught, died, and arose, but yet it was a bitter disappointment. It has been the scene of strife and struggle and barrenness and poverty on every hand. In recent years much has been done to change this condition. I have often been asked why I did not make a trip to the land of Palestine, and have been invited to join parties for a trip to the Holy Land. I have never desired to go at all at this time. My Bible tells me all I need to know about the land during these days of Israel's dispersion. Moreover, I am going to the Holy Land someday anyway, and without any expense, absolutely free, for when Jesus returns to earth all believers will be with Him, and He will come directly to Canaan in Judea before Jerusalem. I can afford to wait until I make that trip of all trips with the Messiah as my Leader and Guide.

The condition of waste and ruin and barrenness which Palestine has presented for these many centuries until just recently was also prophesied many, many years before Israel was driven from the land of promise.

Way back in Leviticus 26:32 God predicted the condition of Palestine during Israel's dispersion: "And I will bring the land into desolation: and your enemies which dwell therein shall be astonished at it."

Or turn to Jeremiah:

> Because my people have forgotten me, they have burned incense to vanity, and they have caused them to stumble in their ways from the ancient paths, to walk in paths, in a way not cast up;
> To make their land desolate, and a perpetual hissing; every one that passeth thereby shall be astonished, and wag his head (Jeremiah 18:15-16).

Or, Jeremiah nineteen verse eight: "And I will make this city desolate, and an hissing; every one that passeth thereby shall be astonished and hiss because of all the plagues thereof."

All of these passages and many more might be multiplied to speak to us of the condition of the land during the dispersion of Israel because of their sin. A question arises. Do any doubt that all this was literally fulfilled? Only a fool can deny it. Then I want to ask frankly, what reason, what argument, have you for saying that the promises spoken by the same prophets concerning the restoration of the whole Twelve Tribes of Israel and the land of Palestine both as regards the northern and the southern kingdom, both Judah and Israel, will not as literally and truly and as surely be fulfiled by the same God? It is a spiritual crime to apply Israel's curses literally because they have been historically fulfilled, and then turn about and spiritualize the promises of their restoration and apply them to someone else. They were all spoken by the same God through the prophets at the same time before any of them had been fulfilled or come to pass. To deal thus with the Word of God is not only violating the clear meaning of Scripture, but a violation of every rule of logic and fairness. Surely, consistency, thou art a jewel.

Therefore, let us believe God as literally when He speaks of Israel's restoration as when He speaks of her dispersion. Here is God's Word so clearly given, that I am sure if you will read it, there will be no question left in your mind.

> And it shall come to pass in that day, that the Lord shall set his hand again the second time to recover the remnant of his people, which shall be left, from Assyria, and from Egypt, and from Pathros, and from Cush and from Elam, and from Shinar, and from Hamath, and from the islands of the sea (Isaiah 11:11).

This same truth is again repeated in Jeremiah thirty-three where we read:

> Thus saith the Lord; If ye can break my covenant of the day, and my covenant of the night, and that there should not be day and night in their season;
>
> Then may also my covenant be broken with David my servant, that he should not have a son to reign upon his throne; and with the Levites the priests, my ministers.
>
> As the hosts of heaven cannot be numbered, neither the sand of the sea measured: so will I multiply the seed of David my servant, and the Levites that minister unto me.
>
> Moreover the word of the Lord came to Jeremiah, saying,
>
> Considerest thou not what this people have spoken, saying, The two families which the Lord hath chosen, he hath even cast them off? thus they have despised my people, that they should be no more a nation before them.
>
> Thus saith the Lord; If my covenant be not with day and night, and if I have not appointed the ordinances of heaven and earth;
>
> Then will I cast away the seed of Jacob, and David my servant, so that I will not take any of his seed to be the rulers over the seed of Abraham, Isaac, and Jacob: for I will cause their captivity to return, and have mercy on them (Jeremiah 33:20-26).

In the closing chapter of the prophecy of Amos we have a statement which cannot possibly be misunderstood.

> And I will bring again the captivity of my people of Israel, and they shall build the waste cities, and inhabit them; and they shall plant vineyards, and drink the wine thereof; they shall also make gardens, and eat the fruit of them.
>
> And I will plant them upon their land, and they shall

no more be pulled up out of their land which I have given them, saith the Lord thy God (Amos 9:14-15).

In this passage we have the promise of the Lord Himself that there will come a time when the nation of Israel shall return to the land of Palestine, and never again be caused to be removed. Some would tell us that all of this was fulfilled in the return of the forty thousand Jews from the captivity in Babylon under Zerubbubel, Nehemiah and Ezra, but will you please notice that those who returned in that time were subsequently again scattered throughout the world and their land laid waste, but Amos tells of a time when they shall return *never* to be scattered again. Since this has never yet occurred in all of Israel's history, it must, therefore, still lie in the future. Consider the closing verses of Amos nine very carefully, because they give God's own Word which cannot be broken concerning the very things we are trying to bring to you.

Do you believe these promises of God? Do you believe that they have been given in order to be literally received? If you do not believe them, then I ask you, How do you know that He keeps His promise in regard to the matter of your salvation? Surely you cannot believe that unless you believe God keeps His promise to the nation of Israel also. I believe with all my heart that God does keep His promises. I believe that He will yet re-gather the nation of Israel and establish it in its land and make Jerusalem and Palestine the praise of all the earth, instead of the storm center of dissension and hatred and strife. Because I believe that God always keeps His Word and always has, I can also believe that the promise He made to me, "Come unto me, all ye that labour and are heavy laden, and I will give you rest" will be kept by Him. I know that I belong to Him. I know that I have eternal life, because God's Word is ever true. Will you trust Him? Will you accept His promise which He gives to you?

We are rapidly approaching that day of which all the

prophets have been speaking. The Lord Jesus will return from heaven and will shout from the air, and the dead in Christ shall rise first and the living believers shall be instantaneously changed and caught up with them to meet the Lord in the air. Then shall follow a period of time upon the earth called the Great Tribulation, a time of purification and preparation for the return of the King of Kings to set up His eternal kingdom upon the earth. After this tribulation period, the Lord will re-gather the nation of Israel into the land of Canaan and establish them forever. He Himself will be King over them. The nations shall be at rest. They shall beat their swords into plowshares, their spears into pruning hooks, and all military establishments will be dismantled. Then the world will enter upon the long-hoped-for, long-prayed-for era of peace and prosperity when Jesus Christ Himself shall reign and have dominion over land and sea, and earth's remotest regions shall His empire be. Are you ready for that day? It is the next event in the program of God.

Chapter Eight

THE RESTORATION OF PALESTINE

For, behold, in those days, and in that time, when I shall bring again the captivity of Judah and Jerusalem,

I will also gather all nations, and will bring them down into the valley of Jehoshaphat, and will plead with them there for my people and for my heritage Israel, whom they have scattered among the nations, and parted my land (Joel 3:1-2).

THE LAND OF PALESTINE about which there is so much difference of opinion today was given by an everlasting covenant to the twelve tribes of Israel. Because of their disobedience they have been out of the land, scattered among the nations, for many centuries, but are soon again to be restored, according to the promise of God. After lying practically waste for two milleniums, recent years have seen a tremendous revival of interest in the return of Israel to Palestine. Millions upon millions of dollars have been invested in the development of the incalculable, fantastic natural resources of the land. Thousands of the seed of Jacob have immigrated to the land until they have the very flower of Jewish cult and culture in Palestine, having been driven by persecution from other lands to the Holy Land.

AGRICULTURE

Agriculturally the land of Palestine has seen the greatest all-time boom. Thousands of acres have been brought under cultivation. Irrigation projects have been made, running into millions upon millions of dollars and scientific agricultural methods are causing the land to produce some of the finest and choicest fruits in all the world. Surely the dry bones are coming together.

EDUCATION

Palestine in the last few years has also become the home of culture, education and intellectual power. The Hebrew University near Jerusalem on Mt. Scopus has on its faculty some of the brightest keenest minds in all the world. These famed professors teaching in this university are largely refugees from other European lands. This university has today over one thousand students, among them one hundred American Jews studying there at the expense of the G. I. Bill of Rights. Surely the bones are beginning to come together again.

In recent years has come the Zionist movement, organized as a world-wide attempt of Jewry led by some of its ablest minds and brains to foster the setting aside of Palestine as a home for the nation of Israel. As a result of this, there is in the land of Palestine, the city of Tel Aviv, an all-Jewish community.

Toward the close of World War I certain events took place which made many earnest Christian students believe that the time of Israel's restoration, according to the promise of God the setting up of the Kingdom and the return of the Messiah, was very, very near. The Allies took Palestine, and General Allenby marched into the city and delivered it from the domination of those who had held it for many, many centuries, It was then that a modest little Jewish chemist who was responsible in a large way for winning the war for the Allies made his wonderful offer to the leaders of Britain. This Jewish scientist, Dr. Chaim Weizmann, who is now president of Palestine, came forward in the hour of apparent defeat for the Allies with a new formula for the most powerful explosive ever discovered up until that time, T.N.T. He donated that discovery to his beloved country, Britain, and that was the one event which did more to turn the tide of victory for the Allies than anything else. This is a matter of history and may be corroborated by referring to your encyclopedia.

It was then Lord Balfour announced that in the event of victory over the enemy the land of Palestine would be set aside and given to the nation of Israel as their national home land—the dream of Zionism. The war did end as a result of this contribution by this Jewish chemist, Dr. Weizmann, and the Balfour Declaration gave Britain the mandate over the land of Palestine. Here, we believe, was Britain's golden opportunity. She now had it in her power and her right to clear the land of its unlawful possessors, and make it exclusively the home land for God's scattered people. All Christendom believed that the time for the restoration had come.

However, for reasons of expediency or otherwise, this dream and this promise was never fully realized. Instead of giving Palestine back to Israel and it being set aside as a home land for the nation, the white paper was issued and the Arabs, the direct descendants of Ishmael, were permitted to remain in the land together with the seed of Isaac, and we have the history of the tent of Abraham repeated again. If only the nations had been able to see their way clear to keep their promise to set aside the Holy Land as a national refuge, and returned it again to the rightful possessors to whom God has promised it, God might have raised many, many more of the seed of Jacob like Dr. Weizmann to bring additional blessing and help to the nations of the world. I am positive in my own mind that had the nations kept their promise, World War II would never have come. If we are on God's side, we will always have a majority.

All of this, of course, is a repetition of the history of the tent of Abraham. Abraham had, among other children, Ishmael, the first-born, and Isaac, who was the son of promise. As long as Ishmael was alone in the tent of Abraham there was no difficulty. But as soon as Isaac, the son of promise, was born to Abraham, God's Word was, "cast out the bondwoman and her son . . . for in Isaac shall thy seed be called." At first Abraham refused, but God made it very clear to him that Isaac and Ishmael could not live in the same tent together.

Isaac was the Father of Israel and Ishmael was the Father of the Ishmaelites. The present day Arabs are the direct descendants of Ishmael, the first-born of Abraham. They were in the land first because Ishmael was born in the tent before Isaac, but God had promised the land, not to him, but to Isaac, the son of the covenant. Historically that experience is being repeated. While the land had been promised as a homeland for the descendants of Isaac through Jacob, there has been trouble in the land ever since, because Ishmael has occupied the land, not only before Isaac's coming, but even after Isaac's re-establishment in the land. The Palestinian problem will continue, until, in obedience to God, the sons of the bondwoman are put out to make way for the sons of promise.

DIVIDING THE LAND

After the default of the Balfour Declaration and failure to set aside all of Palestine as the exclusive, national home land for Israel, probably the greatest mistake of all history

was made. In taking up this tragic error may I state that
we are not trying to be critical in any way, or faultfinding,
but only seeking to set forth the teaching of the Word in
the hope that it may come to the attention of some who
are in a position to do something about it, in order that
God's plan, which can never be ignored, might be carried
out.

In seeking to quiet the unrest in the land of Palestine
and to stop the continual fighting of Jews and Arabs, a
proposal was advanced some years ago to divide the land
into a number of divisions. Recently, this proposal has
been revived and it was suggested to divide the land of
Palestine and split it into three parts; the north part to
be set aside for the Arabs; a part in the south in Judea for
the descendants of Isaac, the Israelites; and the middle part
to be under the nations' control and jurisdiction. Oh, if the
nations only knew what this proposal really means, for
we believe that it marks the beginning, not only of the
end, but one of the saddest periods of human history. The
Word of God is definitely clear that to divide the land
of Palestine is to commit a crime which God will not permit to go unjudged. We remember the protest which went
up from the Zionists all over the world and the strong de-
nunciation from the people of Israel when this proposal
was first put forward. The proposal has not in any way
solved the problem, but the difficulties, on the contrary,
have continued and increased and will do so until we
return to the Word of the Lord.

THE DOUBLE SIN

At the beginning of this chapter we referred to Joel,
chapter three, and we repeat the passage:

> For, behold, in those days, and in that time, when I shall
> bring again the captivity of Judah and Jerusalem,
> I will also gather all nations, and will bring them down

into the valley of Jehoshaphat, and will plead with them there for my people and for my heritage Israel, (now note very, very carefully) whom they have scattered among the nations, and parted (or divided) my land (Joel 3:1-2).

Note very carefully the two reasons why God Himself says He is going to judge the nations of the world. First, because they have scattered His people among the nations. Second, because they have parted or divided His land, and remember that God says, "It is *my* land" and the land refers to the land of Palestine. The first sin, then, which many of the nations have committed, was persecuting and scattering God's people, Israel, and we have seen them go down one after another. The second great error is the partition and cutting up of the Promised Land. We are praying that God will open the eyes of the leaders of the nations, and especially our own beloved nation, that they may have no part in this proposal to divide the land of Palestine. Turn to Daniel, chapter eleven. Here in describing the last act of the antichrist, the man of sin, who will reign in the world after the Rapture of the church, we read this statement:

Thus shall he (that is, the antichrist) do in the most strong holds with a strange god, whom he shall acknowledge and increase with glory: and he shall cause them to rule over many, and shall divide the land for gain (Daniel 11:39).

Then follows immediately the record of God's judgment upon this man of sin, and his ultimate ruin, all because of this particular sin of dividing the land. May I repeat, the judgment of God is pronounced upon the man of sin immediately following the statement that he shall divide the land for gain.

THE LAST STRAW

According to the clear teaching of the Word of God, the next event in the program of God will be the catching away of the Church of the Lord Jesus. Then the man of sin, the antichrist, the antitype of Nimrod, Nebuchad-nezzar and the Caesars will appear on the scene. He will first of all promise the nation of Israel to restore them back again into their land, and when he has by deception gained their confidence, he will turn upon them in the midst of that tribulation period and will, according to Scripture, repeat the sin of dividing the land of Palestine. When he stretches out his hand to touch that which is holy, that which God has called "My land," it will be the last straw, it will be the occasion for the coming of the judgment of the Almighty God upon the man of sin and upon his armies, and upon all his program. He shall be miserably destroyed at the coming of the Lord Jesus Christ in power and in great glory. It is well to remember this because it is taught in type as well as in direct statement throughout all Scripture. Remember that Belshazzar, who was a type of this coming man of sin, made the great mistake of stretching forth his hand to touch the thing which God had called holy. Oh, that we might see the day when the nations would turn over to the true possessors of the land of Palestine their full rights and thereby receive the blessing of the Lord. Let us pray that God may give wisdom to our own leaders that we may not invite the judgment of Almighty God which He has pronounced upon all those who shall touch the things which God has called holy, His people, and His land.

We have taken all of this time and gone into consid-erable detail in order that we might set before you what we believe to be, according to the Word of God, the basic problem of the world today; and the one and only hope for, the longed for and sought for peace for which man is striving. Israel is still God's chosen nation. By this we do not mean that they as individuals can be saved without the Lord Jesus Christ. They too, must come as individual sinners and receive His finished work. We do mean that as a nation, in God's national dealings, they are still His chosen people.

Palestine, the Holy Land, is also still God's chosen land, and there can be no peace in this world until the nation and the land, according to God's purpose, are again fully united. Every effort for peace, all the wisdom and sincerity of diplomats and endless bloodshed will never bring about a government which will assure lasting tranquility and prosperity. Only as the nation of the covenant is back in the covenant land, and the Messiah is their king, will the time come when they shall beat their swords into plowshares and their spears into pruning hooks and they shall learn war no more. The key to lasting peace is the land of Israel and the Israel of the land. The Lord has commanded us to "pray for the peace of Jerusalem: they shall prosper that love thee." When Jerusalem is at peace, the world will be at peace. Let us pray, therefore, that the leaders of the nations and our own nation may see that God is on the side of those who recognize this program. We believe the wars that have been ravaging the world and causing utter destruction of many of the nations which have avowed to exterminate Israel and are seeking to conquer Palestine will ultimately be defeated. Soon the day will be here when the oppressors shall cease, and Christ shall have dominion over land and sea.

We have tried to set before you God's program. Not in vain has He said, "Pray for the peace of Jerusalem: they shall prosper that love thee." The word Jerusalem means "The City of Peace." Basically the meaning is, "The foundation for peace." Notice that the meaning of the word Jerusalem is "The foundation for peace." As long as Jerusalem is not at peace, the world cannot be at peace. Only as Jerusalem is at peace will peace cover the earth. Let us pray that the time may soon come. Let us pray for our leaders. Let us pray for our Nation and the nations of the world that they may recognize God's program, and that the day may soon be ushered in when every man shall sit under his own vine and under his own fig tree, and the nations shall learn war no more. Very, very soon, we believe, from all indications about us, He who said He would come will come. Then we shall see the fulfillment and the vindication of the promises God has made, which man has forgotten, but which will still be fulfilled in every detail.

Chapter Nine

THE BACKSIDE OF THE DESERT

> Now Moses kept the flock of Jethro his father in law, the priest of Midian: and he led the flock to the backside of the desert, and came to the mountain of God, even to Horeb.
>
> And the angel of the Lord appeared unto him in a flame of fire out of the midst of a bush: and he looked, and behold, the bush burned with fire, and the bush was not consumed (Exodus 3:1-2).

The burning bush in the desert which met the eyes of Moses is a miracle, in a book which abounds with miracles, from beginning to end. The book of Exodus is more than the ancient history of a people who were delivered from the land of Egypt and bondage; it is a tremendous revelation of God's eternal providential dealings in the affairs of this world. It is the great miracle book of the Old Testament. It begins with the record of the miracle nation of all time, the nation of Israel, miraculously brought into being, miraculously preserved, though scattered throughout the nations for some twenty-five hundred years. The rest of the book of Exodus is an elaboration of the providence of God in miraculously preserving this miracle nation. It is a prophecy of God's future dealing with this nation until the end of time, and is characterized all along the line by miracle upon miracle.

In Exodus three we have the miracle of the burning bush, then follow the miracles by Moses in Egypt before

King Pharaoh. The Israelites were miraculously delivered
on the Passover night, miraculously led out of Egypt,
miraculously passed through the Red Sea, fed by miracle
bread from heaven, led by a miracle cloud of fire by
night, fed from the miracle-working God with manna and
meat, supplying water from the miracle rock in the wilderness, and healed by the miracle of the brazen serpent.
Miracle after miracle characterizes the whole history of
this amazing nation of Hebrews.

The Lesson of the Bush

One of the greatest miracles of all is the burning bush
on the backside of the desert. To anyone who will take
time to read the context of this passage, it will immediately become crystal clear that this burning bush is
a picture of Israel. It is a picture not only of the Hebrews
at the time of Moses, passing through the fires of persecution in Egypt, supernaturally preserved, but it becomes
also a prophecy of their entire future of wandering among
the nations, of passing through the fires; but never, never
consumed. No better description of the history of this
nation could possibly be given than that of a bush, always burning, but never destroyed. In the midst of the
bush was their Jehovah God, here called the Angel of the
Lord, so that to destroy the nation of the bush would be
as easy as destroying God Almighty Himself.

The Setting of the Bush

In order to understand the lesson of the burning bush
as applied to the nation of Israel we must first of all
acquaint ourselves with the context of our passage and
the setting of this incident on the backside of the desert.
The nation of Israel, the Twelve Tribes of Jacob, had
been in Egypt for some four hundred years as slaves and
serfs of a wicked king who had desperately sought to
get rid of these unwelcome strangers. At first he had
tried to work them to death in the brickyards of Egypt,

but this had failed, so the king tried to get the midwives to kill all the male children as soon as they were born. God intervened miraculously and moved upon the midwives to disobey the king as we read in Exodus 1:17: "But the midwives feared God, and did not as the king of Egypt commanded them, but saved the men children alive."

The next fagot added to the burning bush was a new command of the king. He ordered that all the male Hebrew children should at birth be cast into the river, thinking that if all the male children could be killed in this way, and the female children reduced to slaves, he would entirely rid himself of this nation in a generation or two. God again intervened and Moses was born, spared for three months in the home of his mother, and then put in the ark of bulrushes and laid by the riverside. Again God performed a miracle, for the king's daughter came along and adopted this Hebrew child, whom her father had commanded should be put to death. For forty years Moses was groomed and educated in the court of Pharaoh to be the next king of Egypt, but at the end of those years,

> By faith Moses, when he was come to years, refused to be called the son of Pharaoh's daughter;
> Choosing rather to suffer affliction with the people of God, than to enjoy the pleasures of sin for a season (Hebrews 11:24-25).

As a result, Moses went out to defend his brethren, was rejected and turned down by them, and because of this, forsook his brethren and fled to the backside of the desert. He was trying to forget this ungrateful people for whom he had jeopardized his life, feeling that God too had forgotten them, and here is where God found him after forty years. The time had come for the Hebrew children to be delivered and Moses was God's chosen man for the job. Centuries before, God had already promised that he would deliver Israel at this very time. Here are

God's words spoken to Abraham over four hundred years before,

> And he said unto Abram, Know of a surety that thy seed shall be a stranger in a land that is not theirs and shall serve them; and they shall afflict them four hundred years;
> And also that nation, whom they shall serve, will I judge: and afterward shall they come out with great substance (Genesis 15:13-14).

What a marvelous evidence of the infallible inspiration of the Word of God in which God predicted, four hundred years before it happened, the history of Abraham's seed in Egypt, and fulfilled His Word to the last detail. It is the same God who has also predicted the entire history of the nation of Israel to the very end of time, and is this very moment carrying out all that which He has promised to do by all the prophets, in fulfillment of the message of the burning bush.

When the four hundred years of bondage which God had told Abraham about were almost up God visited Moses in the wilderness on the backside of the desert. The first thing after His visit which greeted Moses' amazed and wondering eyes was the burning bush and out of the bush a voice, the voice of the same One who had spoken to Abraham, saying, "Draw not nigh hither: put off thy shoes from off thy feet, for the place whereon thou standest is holy ground" (Exodus 3:5).

MOSES' LESSON

Moses is to be the deliverer of Israel in fulfillment of God's Word, but before he is ready for the job he must receive some instruction, and his textbook is the burning bush. In essence God says to Moses, "This bush which is burning and not devoured is the nation you have forsaken in Egypt. They are in the fire, burning, burning, burning under the hot sun of Egypt, under the smart of the taskmaster's whip, under the awful cruelty of seeing their children cast to the beasts of the river. But listen, Moses,

I have not forsaken them. Look at this bush. *I am in it and with them,* and if the bush is consumed, I will have to be consumed also, for I am right here in the 'midst of the bush.' Israel shall never perish because of a promise and a covenant which I have made, and from which I can never depart." That truth stands out in the entire passage. Notice these words recorded just before God meets Moses in the bush:

> And it came to pass in process of time, that the king of Egypt died: and the children of Israel sighed by reason of the bondage, and they cried, and their cry came up unto God by reason of the bondage.
>
> And God heard their groaning, and God remembered his covenant with Abraham, with Isaac, and with Jacob.
>
> And God looked upon the children of Israel, and God had respect unto them (Exodus 2:23-25).

Then immediately follows the record in chapter three of the burning bush. The lesson is evident, for God was showing Moses that *he* remembered His covenant with His children even in the fires of affliction. After Moses had stood by the burning bush, God again reminded him of this fact and we read in Exodus 3:5-6:

> And he said, Draw not nigh hither: put off thy shoes from off thy feet, for the place whereon thou standest is holy ground.
>
> Moreover he said, I am the God of thy father, the God of Abraham, the God of Isaac, and the God of Jacob. And Moses hid his face; for he was afraid to look upon God.

PICTURE OF GOD'S PLAN

This then is the very first interpretation of the meaning of the burning bush. The bush represents Israel in the fires of affliction in Egypt, but supernaturally preserved from destruction by the presence of God. This is the primary interpretation.

Scripture should be approached from three different angles. All scripture has only *one primary interpretation,* but it also has many practical applications. We call this important rule of Bible study, the rule of triple approach to the Bible. We should first seek to find, in studying any passage of Scripture, what its primary interpretation is. The context will usually make this perfectly clear. Then having seen the primary lesson or interpretation, we can find one or more, oftentimes many, valuable *practical applications* of the same truth, Thirdly, we will usually find that in addition to the interpretation and the application there is also a very important *prophetic revelation*. All three must be sought and studied to prevent us from being lopsided, top-heavy and overbalanced in our emphasis of the meaning of any passage or doctrine in the Bible.

In the burning bush we have a splendid example of the working of this rule. By interpretation we already indicated God telling Moses that although Israel (represented by the bush) is burning in Egypt, they will never perish because of His covenant with them. By application the burning bush teaches us that all God's people in every age must pass through the fires of testing and persecution, but they too shall never perish because of His New Covenant with them. It is true by application to every Christian believer in this age, that if we belong to Christ we may expect to be persecuted, hated, maligned and misunderstood by the world. That is the unbroken testimony of Scripture.

Jesus said, "In the world ye shall have tribulation: but be of good cheer; I have overcome the world" (John 16:33).

Again He said, that if they have hated me, they will also hate you. The servant is not greater than his Lord. Paul tells us that we must through much tribulation enter into the kingdom of God, and Peter tells us this:

> Beloved, think it not strange concerning the fiery trial which is to try you, as though some strange thing happened unto you:
> But rejoice, inasmuch as ye are partakers of Christ's sufferings (I Peter 4:12-13a).

Jesus said:

> Blessed are ye, when men shall hate you, and when they shall separate you from their company, and shall reproach you, and cast out your name as evil, for the Son of man's sake.
>
> Rejoice ye in that day, and leap for joy: for, behold, your reward is great in heaven (Luke 6:22-23).

In Hebrews we read, "For whom the Lord loveth he chasteneth, and scourgeth every son whom he receiveth" (Hebrews 12:6).

Yes, the path of the Christian is through the fire, but it will all turn out to his good. The history of the disciple who really wants to follow the Lord Jesus all the way is the history of the burning bush, always burning but *not consumed.*

PROPHETIC REVELATION

In addition to the primary interpretation of the burning bush as pointing to the Hebrew's pining in Egypt, and the application to God's children in every age, there is here also a *prophetic revelation.* The burning bush is a picture of the *whole course of Israel's future.* The nation of Israel has been in the fire for milleniums, yet not consumed and we shall see in the following chapters that all of it was prophesied beforehand by the Spirit of God. The bush has burned and burned and burned under Pharaoh of Egypt, Nebuchadnezzar of Babylon, under the Persians, the Greeks and the Romans, under a Hitler and a Mussolini. Recently the bush has burned with renewed vigor as hundreds of thousands of Jews referred to only as D.P.'s (displaced persons), pined away in camps while countless others are struggling for the repossession of their ancient home land. That is the prophetic lesson of the burning bush.

In the next chapter we shall study in detail what the Scriptures have to say about Israel's future in the fire, and their final deliverance. To be informed on the meaning of current events in Europe, in Palestine, and to know what lies ahead in the near future, read your Bible in the light of the burning bush. Keep your eyes on the nation of the bush, Israel, the covenant nation of Jehovah. "Pray for the peace of Jerusalem: they shall prosper that love thee" (Psalms 122:6).

Chapter Ten

THE BURNING BUSH

> And the angel of the Lord appeared unto him (Moses) in a flame of fire out of the midst of a bush: and he looked, and, behold, the bush burned with fire, and the bush was not consumed (Exodus 3:2).

THE BURNING BUSH in the desert which Moses encountered is one of the most graphic pictures of the history of the nation of Israel to be found anywhere in the entire Bible. It represents a nation of people burning almost without interruption in the fires of persecution and affliction, and yet miraculously preserved because in the midst of the bush is One, even the angel of the Lord. Because of an everlasting, unbreakable covenant made with their fathers, Abraham and Isaac and Jacob, He will never permit them to perish, but instead will judge every nation who has ever oppressed or persecuted this people. That this bush plainly represents this Hebrew nation is clear not only from the context in Exodus three, but even more clear from the other reference to the bush in Acts seven. In this chapter, we hear Stephen, the first martyr, giving a brief but wonderfully complete history of the nation of Israel, beginning with Abraham, the first Hebrew. When he comes to the history of Moses, we have him saying in verses 29-32:

> Then fled Moses at this saying, and was a stranger in the land of Madian, where he begat two sons.
> And when forty years were expired, there appeared to

him in the wilderness of mount Sina an angel of the Lord
in a flame of fire in a bush.

When Moses saw it, he wondered at the sight: and as he
drew near to behold it, the voice of the Lord came unto
him,

Saying, I am the God of thy fathers, the God of Abraham,
and the God of Isaac, and the God of Jacob. Then Moses
trembled, and durst not behold. (Acts 7:29-32).

God left no doubt in the mind of Moses as to the message He wished to convey at the burning bush. It is the
nation of Israel which cannot perish as a nation forever,
because of the covenant made with their fathers. God's
plan for the ages centers about this single nation of the
bush, His covenant people. This covenant which God
made with Abraham in behalf of his seed was a covenant
of *grace*, that is, totally independent of the merit, conduct
or worthiness of the nation to whom He made the promise.
It was an unconditional covenant, as all the covenants of
grace are unconditional, in which God promises to do
everything. Read the covenant as stated in Genesis 12,
13, 15 and 17, and later repeated to Isaac, Jacob and
David. There is not a single *if* in it anywhere. God says
over and over *I will, I will, I will*. Moreover, this covenant
was not only an unbreakable covenant, but it was an
everlasting covenant. Here is the statement of the Lord
Himself in Genesis seventeen:

And I will establish my covenant between me and thee
and thy seed after thee in their generations for an everlasting
covenant, to be a God unto thee, and to thy seed after thee.

And I will give unto thee, and to thy seed after thee, the
land wherein thou art a stranger, all the land of Canaan,
for an everlasting possession; and I will be their God
(Genesis 17:7-8).

Surely these words are unmistakable. Two things are to
be noted. First, Abraham will have a seed, and second, the
land of Canaan, better known to us as Palestine, shall be
the *everlasting possession of that seed*. We know the seed
is the nation of Israel, so recently revived again, and the

land is the land of Canaan, which they, according to God's sure Word, will ultimately possess as their everlasting home land. To place any other interpretation on these words is to violate every rule of common sense and consistent Bible study. Now comes the burning bush. Between the giving of this promise and its ultimate fulfillment lie millenniums of time. Instead of the nation of Israel living peacefully and undisturbed in their home land, Canaan, they have been scattered all over the earth, driven from pillar to post and made to pass through the fires of unmentionable persecutions. This too was in the plan and knowledge of God.

About four hundred years after the covenant with Abraham was made, the Lord made another covenant with Abraham's seed, the nation of Israel, just delivered out of Egypt. This covenant was made at Sinai and was the covenant of the Law. It was given to Moses for Israel and Israel exclusively. This second covenant was of *works* and the blessing of this covenant was conditioned upon *their behavior* and their *obedience*. If they obeyed, blessing would follow, if they were disobedient, the curse would follow. But man, fallen man, cannot keep God's holy Law, and so Israel failed under this Sinaitic covenant of works, and as a result, His judgment fell upon them, they were driven from their land and scattered among the nations for these past twenty-five hundred years. All this was prophesied even before they entered the land.

> And I will scatter you among the nations, and will draw out a sword after you: and your land shall be desolate, and your cities waste.
> And ye shall perish among the nations . . . (Leviticus 26:33, 38).

Remember these words were spoken by God *years before* the Israelites had even entered the land of Palestine, and these words stand as one of the greatest evidences of the inspiration of Scripture. What minute detail God gives as to all which should befall this nation. As we read history, we marvel without ceasing at the accuracy and infallibility of this Word in describing beforehand the entire course of the history of the nation of the *burning bush*.

We might go on indefinitely quoting from the entire Bible to show how the Scriptures predict that, because of Israel's disobedience, they would be cast into the fires of persecution and become indeed history's *burning bush*. But here comes the miracle, and the place where so many Christians make their *big mistake*. They imagine that because Israel broke the covenant of the law, God nullifies His covenant of grace with Abraham. So there are millions of people, Christian people, who think God is all through with Israel as a nation, and that it will never return to the land of Palestine as a nation again. So these Scriptures are either passed over and ignored, or made symbolic and spiritualized to make them apply to the church as spiritual Israel, and all the covenants and promises are taken away from the poor despised and dispersed nation of Israel and given to the church. But even though *man is unfaithful, God* never fails to keep his promises and He who said to Abraham, "And I will give unto thee, and to thy seed after thee, the land wherein thou art a stranger, all the land of Canaan, for an everlasting possession" will never change.

It is still as true today as it was then. Abraham believed it literally, Isaac did, Jacob did, and David and Solomon, and the prophets and Paul, and so do the thousands of Bible believing Israelites who today are struggling to regain their lost land of Palestine. God will not, cannot break His covenant. The bush may burn, but it can never perish. There are verses in Galatians which should forever settle this matter. Paul is discussing in Galatians the truth of God's grace and showing that God never goes back on His Word: that even though His people may be ever so unfaithful and disobedient, God keeps His promise. To illustrate this truth, Paul goes back into the history of God's dealing with the nation of Israel and says,

> And this I say, that the covenant, that was confirmed before of God in Christ, the law, which was four hundred and thirty years after, cannot disannul, that it should make the promise of none effect.
>
> For if the inheritance be of the law, it is no more of promise: but God gave it to Abraham by promise (Galatians 3:17, 18).

Do not hurry over that passage, for it is all important in the understanding of the burning bush. According to Paul the covenant of grace made with Abraham concerning his seed, that they should never cease to be a nation, and that the land of Canaan was to be their everlasting possession, remains entirely *unaffected* by the fact of Israel's disobedience and their subsequent scattering among the nations for all these centuries. Read the passage again slowly and carefully. Paul in Romans corroborates this truth when he says,

> I say then, Hath God cast away his people? (Israel) God forbid. For I also am an Israelite, of the seed of Abraham, of the tribe of Benjamin.
>
> God hath not cast away his people which he foreknew (Romans 11:1-2).

In verse 25 of the same chapter Paul clinches the matter once and for all and informs us,

> For I would not, brethren, that ye should be ignorant of this mystery, lest ye should be wise in your own conceits; that blindness in part is happened to Israel, until the fulness of the Gentiles be come in.
>
> And so all Israel shall be saved: as it is written, There shall come out of Zion the Deliverer, and shall turn away ungodliness from Jacob:
>
> For this is my covenant unto them, when I shall take away their sins (Romans 11:25-27).

Yes, the Lord will save Israel and bring them back into the land of their fathers, according to God's covenant which cannot be broken.

THE UP-TO-DATE APPLICATION

This is the lesson of the burning bush: Israel in the fires of affliction, but miraculously preserved. Then God raises up Moses and after a brief time in which God sends plagues and judgments upon Egypt, they all are delivered and all return to their land, and "not an hoof is left behind." I wonder how many realize that we are standing this very moment, prophetically, where Moses stood historically on that day on the backside of the desert. For Egypt is the type of the nations afflicting Israel. God has not forgotten His people and in the past raised up Moses. Moses is only a type of the "prophet greater than Moses," the Messiah of Israel who will soon come in fulfillment of all prophecy and the promise of Abraham and will once again lead them out of their bondage into their own land. That time is prophetically here. No other nation has been so much in the news as Israel. No other land has been so prominent in the news as Canaan. The years of bondage for Israel are about over. Soon the Messiah will come. First He will take out His bride, the Church, just as Moses received a Gentile bride in the wilderness while Israel was in bondage; then for a brief time the bush will burn with its most intense heat, the Time of Jacob's Trouble, called the Tribulation and the Day of the Lord. After this brief period of great tribulation, represented by the last burning of the bush, Israel's Moses, their Messiah, the Lord Jesus, will return to them, thoroughly judge their oppressors and their enemies, and then bring them back into the land of their fathers according to His sure Word, so beautifully given in Isaiah ten:

> For though thy people Israel be as the sand of the sea, yet a remnant of them shall return: the consumption decreed shall overflow with righteousness.
>
> For the Lord God of hosts shall make a consumption, even determined, in the midst of all the land.

Therefore thus saith the Lord God of hosts, O my people that dwellest in Zion, be not afraid of the Assyrian: he shall smite thee with a rod, and shall lift up his staff against thee, after the manner of Egypt (Isaiah 10:22-24).

Or hear what Jeremiah says,

Therefore they shall come and sing in the height of Zion, and shall flow together to the goodness of the Lord, for wheat, and for wine, and for oil, and for the young of the flock and of the herd: and their soul shall be as a watered garden; and they shall not sorrow any more at all (Jeremiah 31:12).

Chapter Eleven

THE COMING REDEEMER

IN THE STORY OF MOSES, the nation of Egypt is a type of the nations of the world. The burning bush is a picture of Israel among these nations afflicted and oppressed but supernaturally preserved by Almighty God, because of the covenant made with their fathers. Moses is a type of the coming Redeemer Messiah, who after the last burning of the bush in the great Tribulation will deliver His people and settle them for ever in their promised land of Canaan. The literal burning bush in the desert is history, the *lesson* of the burning bush is prophecy. As the bush could not be destroyed, but was preserved, one day to be laden with fruit, so too Israel is the indestructible nation. This is not only asserted by God in His Word, but 2500 years of history have abundantly proven it. Pharaoh could not drown them, Nebuchadnezzar could not burn them, the lions would not eat them, the whale could not digest them, and Haman could not hang them. They are the burning bush, indestructible for the "bush burned with fire, and the bush was not consumed."

MOSES WAS A TYPE OF CHRIST

Moses, Israel's deliverer, is one of the many glorious types of the coming Redeemer of Israel, their Messiah and their King, who shall one day, like Moses, deliver them from the nations among whom they have been scattered and restore them back into their own land, never to be plucked up again. Moses' life, as the type of this coming Redeemer, is divided into three well and sharply defined periods as follows:

1. The period of preparation in the king's house (forty years).

2. The period of rejection in the wilderness (forty years).

3. The period of deliverance and emancipation. (forty years).

For forty years Moses was in the king's house so that he was prepared for that great day when he should appear before the king to plead the cause of his brethren, the children of Israel. There he was instructed in all the rules and regulations of the royal court and learned all about the proper court procedure and etiquette, so that he and he alone was able later to enter the king's presence.

Jesus, too, the Messiah of Israel and the Saviour of his people, like Moses, spent an eternity in the house of the great King of heaven and earth. "In the beginning was the Word, and the Word was with God, and the Word was God," is the testimony of John in the first chapter of the Gospel through John. Then in the fullness of time Jesus came forth and was born nineteen hundred years ago as a babe in Bethlehem and offered Himself to His people Israel as their Saviour and Deliverer, but like Moses He was rejected the first time He came. "He came unto His own, and His own received Him not." So He left them and has been in the wilderness of Israel's rejection for these nineteen hundred years. While He is in rejection he receives a Gentile bride, and one day, like Moses, He is coming back the second time. Then the nation which rejected Him the first time will own Him and receive Him and He will deliver them and lead them into the land of promise, the land of Canaan, never to be plucked up or removed again.

JOSEPH IS ALSO A TYPE OF CHRIST

We also have the very same picture in the life of Joseph, another clear and unmistakable type of the Lord Jesus the Messiah. Joseph, too, was raised in his father's house as his own beloved son. He, too, was sent to visit his brethren, but they refused him and rejected him. They sold him into the hands of the Gentiles for twenty pieces of silver. He went away to be exalted to the right hand of the king of Egypt and when the great famine came, he appeared to them the second time and was accepted by them, became their deliverer and brought them into the land of plenty. While he was in rejection by his brethren, he also received a Gentile Bride in Egypt, who was destined to reign with him on the throne.

KING DAVID ALSO WAS A TYPE OF CHRIST

What was true of Joseph and Moses was true in the case of another outstanding type of the Messiah in the Old Testament. David was God's choice of king for Israel. When he came unto Israel the first time as their king they rejected him, and followed a false king, Saul, type of the antichrist, and David was caused to flee into the land of the Philistines, to remain there, rejected of his brethren. While out of the land and disowned by his people, David too received a Gentile bride, after which he returned to his people a second time, was received by them and became their king and established them in the land. And so we might go on, for the Bible is full of these wonderful typical and prophetic pictures of the One of whom Joseph, Moses and David were only types.

Of course, without the New Testament revelation we could never have seen these significant shadows of the coming Redeemer, but now with the light of the entire Bible we see the magnificent wonderful harmony of the Scriptures, which speak of *Him* from cover to cover. It reminds me of a bit of advice an old preacher gave me when I first began my ministry. He said, "My son, if you ever find certain Scriptures that you just cannot understand or interpret, try putting the Lord Jesus right in the center of those passages and see how they begin to have meaning." I have tried that thing time and time again and have never found it to fail. Even in the historical passages, and even in the geneologies, if you look closely, you will find Him somewhere to lighten up the whole passage. We can never fully understand the Old Testament, until the light of His face is made to shine upon it, for all the Scriptures speak of Him. Jesus Himself asserted this when speaking to the two disciples on the way to Emmaus after His resurrection. We read this record in Luke 24:27, Jesus speaking, "And beginning at Moses and all the prophets, he expounded unto them in all the scriptures the things concerning himself."

The Scriptures Jesus referred to were the *Old Testament Scriptures,* for not a single book of the New Testament was written at that time. If you then really want to understand the Bible you must keep Jesus Christ in the midst of all of it, and realize that directly or indirectly all the Scriptures have this one aim and puropse, to reveal *Him,* the Son of God, the Son of man, the Messiah of Israel and the Saviour of the world. This is wonderfully true in the case of Moses. His whole ministry is a shadow and picture, unmistakably clear, of the Lord Messiah who is coming again the second time to deliver His people. Today He is in heaven rejected as King, at the right hand of God, waiting for the signal to return and fulfill every prediction and promise in the word of God, and to culminate the final accomplishment of all that was promised in the covenant which God made with Abraham, Isaac, Jacob, and the children of Israel.

WHEN WILL HE COME?

Since all of the above is true, we are naturally deeply interested in the question, When will He come again?

He came the first time nineteen hundred years ago, according to the promise of the Old Testament, and He is coming again some day, according to the promise of both the Old and the New Testaments. While we cannot know the day or the hour, and we would not for a single moment engage in date setting and bring the whole truth of prophecy into reproach, the Bible nevertheless does tell us that we may know the times and the seasons (I Thessalonians 5:1-15). There are many many signs of His coming in the Scriptures, but there is one which seems to stand out above the rest. It is the sign of the burning bush.

When the time for Moses' second coming to Israel drew near and the time had come for God to deliver the nation of Israel he indicated it by this *sign,* the burning bush. Remember the bush is Israel in the fire of tribulations, and God speaks to Moses out of the bush, and notice carefully what God's message to Moses was. It is significant.

> And the Lord said, I have surely seen the affliction of my people which are in Egypt, and have heard their cry by reason of their taskmasters; for I know their sorrows;
>
> And I am come down to deliver them out of the hand of the Egyptians, and to bring them up out of that land unto a good land and large, unto a land flowing with milk and honey. . . (Exodus 3:7-8).

I trust you see the significance of these words. The time of the deliverance of the Israelites was near, and God revealed it in the burning bush. The bush on fire becomes the signal for the return of Moses to the land of Egypt to deliver God's covenant nation. That is true today. The signal for the return of the Lord is again the nation of Israel passing through the experience of the burning bush.

During the past few decades, but especially the last few years, all of us have been filled with horror at the reports of the terrible persecutions of this nation throughout the world. The indescribable atrocities under Hitler in Germany and in Italy, not to mention many others, in which millions of this nation were killed and persecuted, banished and left to die in concentration camps, is but the fulfillment of the burning bush over again. The bush is once more ablaze, fed and fanned by those who know not the Lord nor His Word, and the plight of millions of the nation of Israel today is a repetition of their experience of their bondage in Egypt. Thank God, it is also the burning bush. The plight of Israel is and remains the most positive sign of the nearness of the return of their deliverer, the Messiah, the prophet greater than Moses. God's clock is running on time and the hour is soon to strike and His promise cannot be broken, but will soon be fulfilled as He said in all the prophets. Now for the first time in history Israel is again a nation in the land and recognized once more as Israel.

THREE TREES IN SCRIPTURE

The increased interest in and activity concerning the nation of Israel is one of the surest signs of their deliverance and the return of the Lord. This is in harmony with many other figures in the Bible. There are at least three trees in Scripture which are all pictures of Israel. They are the vine mentioned in Isaiah five, the fig tree mentioned by Jesus in Matthew 24:32, Mark 13:28, Luke 21:29 and finally the olive tree as mentioned by Paul in Romans eleven. These three trees are pictures of the same thing as taught in the burning bush. In the case of the vine it was fruitless, but still the vine of the Lord, for Isaiah tells us in Isaiah 5:7: "For the vineyard of the Lord of hosts is the house of Israel, and the men of Judah his pleasant plant."

The vine is passing through the burning and without

fruit but, as we shall see later, is to be restored and fill the face of the earth with fruit. The same lesson we have in the fig tree in the Gospels, the tree cursed by the Lord because it had leaves, but no fruit, but as Jesus taught so clearly, when the fig tree again begins to blossom and bud it will be the sign of their restoration and the coming again of Christ. In perfect harmony with this is the olive tree of Romans eleven. Here the natural branches are broken off and they pass through the burning but only temporarily, for Paul assures us: "And they also, if they abide not still in unbelief, shall be graffed in: for God is able to graff them in again" (Romans 11:23).

All three of these are summed up, as it were, in the burning bush. In the original the word for bush in Exodus three is *bramble bush* or briar bush. A prickly briar bush all aflame, but never destroyed, for God is in the bush. Moses is warned to stay his distance, to take off the shoes from his feet and not to approach this bush, because God and God alone is dealing with it. Oh, that the nations and men would learn the lesson to leave Israel alone, for everyone who touches her, touches the apple of the Lord's eye. Way back in Genesis God said to Abraham, the father of this nation, "And I will bless them that bless thee, and curse him that curseth thee" (Genesis 12:3).

History has proven the truth of this statement, for no nation from Pharaoh on down has ever oppressed that nation and escaped the judgment of God, and vice versa, every nation which has ever protected and sheltered her has been blessed. Today the bush is burning with new fury, but it is only again the sure sign of Israel's early deliverance. May God grant us grace to properly interpret all these events in the light of His promise, to keep our hands off God's chosen nation and "Pray for the peace of Jerusalem."

Soon the King will be here and the church will be

snatched away, and then the last great burning, the Time of Jacob's Trouble, will set in, after which He will return to set up His kingdom and,

> Jesus shall reign where'er the sun
> Doth his successive journeys run;
> His Kingdom stretch from shore to shore,
> Till moons shall wax and wane no more.

Chapter Twelve

THE WAY OF THE BACKSLIDER

WHILE WE ARE DEALING PRIMARILY in this volume with the program of God for the nation of Israel, their past blessing in the land, their present dispersion, and their future restoration, we want to make these messages practical as well as informative. While dealing, therefore, with the burning bush, we insert here some practical lessons for ourselves as suggested by the experience of Moses on the backside of the desert.

> Now Moses kept the flock of Jethro his father in law, the priest of Midian: and he led the flock to the backside of the desert, and came to the mountain of God, even to Horeb.
>
> And the angel of the Lord appeared unto him in a flame of fire out of the midst of a bush: and he looked, and, behold, the bush burned with fire, and the bush was not consumed.
>
> And Moses said, I will now turn aside, and see this great sight, why the bush is not burnt.
>
> And when the Lord saw that he turned aside to see, God called unto him out of the midst of the bush, and said, Moses, Moses. And he said, Here am I.
>
> And he said, Draw not nigh hither: put off thy shoes from off thy feet, for the place whereon thou standest is holy ground (Exodus 3:1-5).

IN THIS PASSAGE FROM EXODUS we have a most remarkable incident, when we remember that it was Moses himself who wrote this record of his own sojourn on the backside of the desert, in a backslidden condition, while his own people of Israel were being ground to pieces in their terrible bondage in the land of Egypt. The fact that Moses records his own sad failure is in itself a great evidence of the inspiration of the Scriptures. Men do not naturally write an autobiography of their failures, but instead are eager and zealous to record their successes. Not so with the Bible; it gives the record of its heroes as well as its villains in all candidness, and without prejudice or bias. In this respect the Bible is unique among all the literature of the ages.

THE BIBLE IS AN HONEST BOOK

The Bible treats all of its characters with equal candor and frankness. It does not exaggerate the evils of the wicked nor does it minimize the mistakes of the faithful. How unlike we are in this respect. When we write a biography or a history we always, consciously or unconsciously, favor our heroes and friends and debase the villain. We exaggerate and play up the virtues of the hero, and carefully omit his vices and sins, while we multiply the weaknesses of the villain, but fail to mention what little good there may even be in their characters.

However, this is not true of the Bible. It is fair to all its subjects and characters. Even the devil is given his just due. The Bible is never influenced by human prejudices or favoritisms. If the Scriptures were written by mere men without the inspiration of the Holy Spirit, this could never have been true, but the fact that the writers of the Bible record with equal honesty the history of the good as well as the evil, is the mark of divine authorship and inspiration. Take for instance the case of Noah. He was the one man who found grace with his family in the days of the flood, and is called a "righteous man." But the same Spirit hesitates not to mention the fact of Noah's drunkenness at the end of his otherwise illustrious career. The Bible calls Abraham the friend of God, but does not shrink from giving an account of his awful failures in not trusting God—as seen in his flight to Egypt, his affair with Hagar the Egyptian, and the birth of Ishmael. The Bible calls David the man after God's own heart, but also relates with biting judgment his terrible sin of murder and adultery. And so we might go on and on. No other writers but the inspired writers of the Bible could have written such a book.

MOSES WAS NO EXCEPTION

The case in point which we have in our Scripture for this message is that of Moses, the writer of the book of Exodus. While he is writing about himself he is compelled by the Holy Spirit, for whom Moses acted only as a stenographer, to write this sad and unhappy record of his forty years out of the will of God, in a backslidden condition on the backside of the desert. Moses, a man who had been groomed to be the next king of Egypt, who had received the most complete and efficient education in the world in the court of Egypt, spending his time shepherding a flock of sheep on the backside of the desert. Moses, who was called to be the great emancipator of the nation of Israel, fleeing like a coward to the place of inactivity and fruitlessness in the desert. The fact that God overruled his backsliding and made this desert experience the means of his preparation to lead Israel through this same wilderness reveals the marvelous matchless grace of God in being willing to use such poor, unworthy instruments as we are.

HOW DID MOSES GET THERE?

To understand the teaching of the Spirit in this incident in the life of Moses, we must go back some forty years in his life and see *why* Moses left the glories and honor of Egypt to seclude himself as an obscure shepherd in the desert. Forty years prior to the record of our text Moses was the chief prince in the house of Pharaoh, king of Egypt, then the most powerful and wealthiest kingdom in all the earth. Tradition tells us and the Bible confirms the fact by its silence, that Pharaoh, the king in Moses' time, had no son to be his heir. He seems to have had one daughter, however, who found little Moses as an infant at the river's brink and had adopted him as her son, thus making Moses the direct heir to the throne of Egypt. For forty years Moses had been educated and groomed for this highest position on the earth so that when Pharaoh died he would become the king of practically the whole world. The writer of Acts tells us something of his thorough preparation, for Stephen says in Acts 7:22 that Moses: "was learned in all the wisdom of the Egyptians, and was mighty in words and in deeds."

Apparently Moses had no desire to be the King of the commonwealth of Egypt, for his heart was with his brethren, the children of Israel, who had been reduced to abject slavery and ignominious servitude by the king. During all those years, while Moses lolled in ease and lived in the most luxurious splendor as the heir apparent to the throne, his heart was with his people. This is very very evident from the record. When he was forty years old he felt the time had come to do something for his people. Here is the informative record:

> By faith Moses, when he was come to years, refused to be called the son of Pharaoh's daughter;
> Choosing rather to suffer affliction with the people of God, than to enjoy the pleasures of sin for a season:
> Esteeming the reproach of Christ greater riches than the treasures in Egypt (Hebrews 11:24-26).

By faith Moses refused to be called the son of Pharaoh's Daughter. All the time, for forty full years, while Moses was being groomed to be the king of Egypt, he had no intention of ever becoming such, but was determined that he would fulfill the commission to which he knew the Lord had called him, to be the redeemer and deliverer of this downtrodden people, his brethren, the children of Israel. He was only biding his time until he felt the hour had come to strike. One day, when Moses was forty years old, he felt that the time had finally come and he went forth with the deliberate and planned purpose of revealing himself to Israel as their emancipator and savior. The Bible definitely states this to be so. In Acts 7:23-25 Stephen, in his address before the Sanhedrin, tells us clearly:

> And when he (Moses) was full forty years old, it came into his heart (Moses) to visit his brethren the children of Israel.
>
> And seeing one of them suffer wrong, he defended him, and avenged him that was oppressed, and smote the Egyptian:
>
> For he (Moses) supposed his brethren would have understood how that God by his hand would deliver them: but they understood not.

It is very important that we bear this fact in mind, in order that we may understand Moses' feelings a little later when he is rejected by the very ones whom he came to deliver. This will explain the surprise and chagrin of Moses when they turned upon him, and it will explain why Moses fled to the backside of the desert.

How Did Moses Know He was to Deliver Israel?

One thing is perfectly evident. Moses *knew* that he was God's man to deliver Israel. He refused to accept the kingship of Egypt, and he deliberately chose to cast his lot with the despised and downtrodden nation of Israel. To reveal himself to it he had gone out and defended one of his brethren, had slain an Egyptian, hoping that the incident would be accepted as his official declaration of his willingness to deliver Israel. Instead, the very ones whom he came to deliver rejected him and turned upon him, as is given so strikingly in Exodus 2:13-15:

> And when he went out the second day. (that was the day after he had declared himself and slain the Egyptian), behold, two men of the Hebrews strove together: and he said to him that did the wrong, Wherefore smitest thou thy fellow?

And he said, Who made thee a prince and a judge over us? intendest thou to kill me, as thou killedst the Egyptian? And Moses feared, and said, Surely this thing is known.

Now when Pharaoh heard this thing, he sought to slay Moses. But Moses fled from the face of Pharaoh, and dwelt in the land of Midian: and sat down by a well.

One must needs put one's self in the position of Moses to understand his hasty departure from Egypt. While the record says that he feared and sought to escape death at the hands of the king, there was another deeper and more serious motive for fleeing. The writer of Hebrews gives us the following interesting sidelight on this incident when he says in Hebrews 11:27: "By faith he forsook Egypt, not fearing the wrath of the king."

Notice the words, *He forsook Egypt not fearing the wrath* of the king. That might have been a secondary motive, but the real reason he fled was undoubtedly his thorough and bitter disappointment with the children of Israel who had rejected his offer to deliver them, for we have already quoted the words of Scripture that Moses "supposed his brethren would have understood how that God through his hand would have delivered them: but they understood not."

This was just too much for poor Moses. Here he had deliberately jeopardized his high position in the court of Pharaoh, had offered to identify himself with this despised people, had declared himself as one with them. Instead of appreciating such sacrifice and devotion, and rallying around him, they had rejected him, turned upon him, and threatened him. This was too much for poor Moses. I can just hear him saying. "Well, of all things, of all the ingratitude and unthankfulness. What do you know about that? Here I have done all this for them, and placed my own life in the balance and this is what I get. That settles it. I am all done, all through with such a bunch of ingrates. They don't deserve any consideration; let them grovel and slave and die in Egypt, that is all they deserve. As far as I am concerned, I am all through now, once and forever. Good-bye, you miserable ingrates." And away Moses went and kept on going till he reached the backside of the desert, as far away as he was able to get from them.

WHERE ARE YOU DWELLING?

For forty long years he dwelt in the desert. Forty years of wasted life, although God overruled it. But as far as rewards, those years were wasted. The Bible tells us very little of those forty years, except that Moses married the daughter of Jethro. During all those forty years the Holy Spirit found nothing to record as being of lasting value in his life. They are a blank, a long period of barren years *on the backside* of the desert. We, of course, can sympathize with Moses, but surely we cannot justify him. All of us who have been called to Christian work can appreciate Moses' feelings and experience. But all this is written for us as a warning that we might not make the mistake of Moses.

If a man is in the work of the Lord for the appreciation and gratitude he expects to receive from men, even from many of God's people, he might better quit before he starts. How often we experience what Moses felt. The very people we have done the most for are too often the very ones who turn upon us at the least provocation. Many a minister of the Gospel and Christian worker is today on the backside of the desert driven from the path of duty and service into the lean desert pastures of the backside of the desert, just because he expected appreciation from men instead of what God promised, persecution and tribulation. Let me repeat, we must expect to be misunderstood and hated and rejected by the very ones we try to help the most. God has not promised His servants an easy path, but to be a disciple of the Lord means the garden of Gethsemane and the Cross. "If any man would be my disciple," said Jesus, "let him follow me."

Where are you dwelling this very moment? Are you on the backside of the desert? You, too, used to be active and busy in the church and Christian work. Now you are on the side lines, criticizing and fault finding, your joy gone. Oh, I know your excuse. Moses had one too, plenty of them in fact, when God finally met him at the burning bush. God remembered Moses, and finally met him. The Lord is calling you, too, back to the place of joy and service. Won't you, poor, unhappy, backslidden Christian, hear His call now and abandon your excuses, admit you have gotten your eyes off the Lord and on men, and repent for your lack of courage and faith and return now to the place of fellowship and joy? "If we confess our sins, he is faithful and just to forgive us our sins, and to cleanse us from all unrighteousness" (I John 1:9).

Chapter Thirteen

A MOTHER'S INFLUENCE

> Now Moses kept the flock of Jethro his father inlaw, the priest of Midian: and he led the flock to the backside of the desert, and came to the mountain of God, even to Horeb (Exodus 3:1).

MOSES, A PRINCE, HEIR APPARENT TO THE THRONE OF Egypt, educated, refined and cultured, called of God to be the great emancipator of the chosen people, the nation of Israel, *on the backside of the desert* feeding a little flock of sheep. Moses, a child of God, the greatest Old Testament character, and type of the coming Redeemer, waiting forty years on the backside of the desert, because he had become disgusted with his friends and his brethren who had repaid his kindness with sneers, and his offer to be their deliverer with a most unkind, ungracious rejection. The sting of this rejection was all the more painful and their treatment of him all the more bitter because Moses knew that he was *God's* man and called of the Lord to be the deliverer of the nation of Israel.

MOSES KNEW HIS CALL

We pointed out in the last chapter that Moses knew he had been called of God for the job of leading the children of Israel out of Egypt. The Bible leaves no doubt on this matter. Stephen says in his address before the Sanhedrin in Acts 7:23, 24:

And when he was full forty years old, it came into his heart to visit his brethren, the children of Israel:

And seeing one of them suffer wrong, he defended him, and avenged him that was oppressed, and smote the Egyptian.

Here follows a very important commentary by the Holy Spirit through Stephen on the motive of Moses in smiting and killing the Egyptian: "For he supposed his brethren would have understood how that God by his hand would deliver them: but they understood not (Acts 7:23-25).

The writer of Hebrews corroborates this statement of Stephen that Moses knew full well his mission and relationship to his enslaved brethren, even though he was the prince of the kingdom of Egypt:

By faith Moses, when he was come to years, refused to be called the son of Pharaoh's daughter,

Choosing rather to suffer affliction with the people of God, than to enjoy the pleasures of sin for a season;

Esteeming the reproach of Christ greater riches than the treasures of Egypt: for he had respect unto the recompence of the reward.

By faith he forsook Egypt, not fearing the wrath of the king (Hebrews 11:24-27).

WHERE DID MOSES GET INFORMATION CONCERNING HIS CALL?

Before we visit poor Moses on the backside of the desert to where he had fled upon his rejection by his own people, we want to inquire into a very important matter, namely, where did Moses get this information concerning his call and commission to be the deliverer of the children of Israel? Remember that Moses was raised in the house of Pharaoh the Egyptian, the cruel relentless oppressor of the children of Israel. Certainly he had not been taught in Pharaoh's house to befriend these despised Hebrews, these despicable slaves. Instead we may rest assured that his education in the court and the schools of Egypt included definite instructions for the continued oppression and ultimate annihilation of this hated race of Hebrews. In spite of all this drilling and teaching, Moses knew and was convinced that his job was not ruling Egypt, but delivering the nation of Israel. Where then did he get his knowledge concerning his work?

FROM HIS MOTHER

While the Bible does not give us the details, it nevertheless gives us enough of a hint in regard to this question so that we can know how God communicated this knowledge to Moses. He could have gotten it nowhere else, than during those very first few years of his life while he was still under the influence and teaching of his godly mother.

AMRAM AND JOCHEBED

The child Moses was a child of prayer. He had two godly parents whose names, I fear, are unknown to the great majority of Bible students. And yet, while ninety-nine out of one hundred people do not even know the names of Moses' parents, and they are just two obscure simple believers, their influence upon the great emancipator Moses is one of the most inspiring chapters in the whole Bible. Moses had been dedicated to the work of the Lord even before he was born. His mother's name was Jochebed and his father's name was Amram, meaning "the exalted one" (Exodus 6:18). The name Jochebed means "God's glory" (Exodus 6:20). Even their names indicate their character. These parents of Moses were God-fearing people who knew the word and the promises of God and were looking for the deliverance of the nation of Israel. God had promised to Abraham that after about four hundred years of bondage in Egypt, his offspring, the nation of Israel, would be delivered from the oppressor. Moses' parents were undoubtedly familiar with this promise in Genesis 15:13-15. God said to Abraham:

> Know of a surety that thy seed shall be a stranger in a land that is not theirs, and shall serve them; and they shall afflict them four hundred years;
> And also that nation, whom they shall serve, will I

judge: and afterward shall they come out with great
substance.

There can be no question that the parents of Moses
knew this prophecy and promise which God had made to
Abraham. When they were expecting the birth of their
child, they hoped that he might be the one through whom
the Lord would bring all this to pass. They knew that the
four hundred years were about up and the time had
come for the deliverance of the nation of Israel. What
greater desire could these parents have than that their
child, in case it were a boy, should be God's chosen instrument for this great task? Therefore, they dedicated
their unborn son to God for this task and *believed* that
God would fulfill and grant their desire. When Moses was
born, God gave them the assurance that he (Moses) was
the one whom He would use and the parents of Moses
acted accordingly. Instead of casting the boy into the
river as all the other male children of these slaves had
been, they hid him for three months and then committed
him to the Lord in the full assurance that God would fulfill His promise through him. All this is clearly suggested
in the record. Moses himself tells us:

> And the woman (his mother) conceived, and bare a
> son: and when she saw that he was a goodly child, she hid
> him three months (Exodus 2:2).

The meaning in the original indicates that she saw that
he was the goodly child, the one whom they had dedicated
to the Lord, and so she hid him *by faith,* and not through
any fear of the king. In this connection it is interesting to
read the New Testament commentary on this passage.
Stephen in speaking to the Sanhedrin in Acts 7:20 says
this: "In which time Moses was born, and was exceeding
fair."

The original Greek means (as you will see in the mar-
ginal note) that he was *"God's fair one."* He was God's
fair one, the one whom God had chosen. Moses' parents

recognized him as God's man in answer to their prayer of faith and therefore hid him three months. Let me repeat, they did not hide him for fear of the king, but through faith in God's promise. If there be any doubt in your mind concerning this, let me refer you to Hebrews 11:23:

> By faith Moses, when he was born, was hid three months of his parents, because they saw that he was a (the) proper child; and they were not afraid of the king's commandment.

Notice that *they were not afraid of the king's commandment. By faith they hid him.*

Notice how God rewards such faith. When they could no longer hide him, when they had done all their part, they left the rest with the Lord and put Moses in an ark of bulrushes and left him at the river's brink. And then God acted. He put in the heart of the king's daughter a desire to go once again to the swimming pool of her childhood days. God placed in her heart pity and compassion for this castaway Hebrew baby, and instead of throwing him into the river, this proud Egyptian princess adopted a despised and hated baby of an enslaved nation. How wonderfully God honors faith when we are only willing to trust Him. The rest of the story is even more intriguing. Moses' sister, witnessing all this, offered to get a nurse for the baby. The mother of Moses was called and her faith was rewarded by receiving her baby whom she had given to the Lord back again and getting paid from the royal treasury for nursing her own baby.

How Long was Moses at Home?

We do not know how long Moses remained in the home of his parents before he was taken in the court of Pharaoh to be groomed for the throne of Egypt. It may have been only a few years, but it was long enough for God to accomplish His purpose of teaching and instructing little Moses by his parents in the task to which they had dedicated him. Here is the answer, then, to the question we raised at the beginning of this chapter, "Where did Moses get his information concerning his mission and his calling to be the deliverer of Israel?" He got it from his father and at his mother's knee during that brief time they had him under their care. During those tender, formative years, he received the most essential and most important training and instruction in the world, the training of the *home,* the instruction at mother's knee. What he learned, let us say, before he was five years old, was never forgotten, but forty years later he still remembered it.

I can just see Jochebed, Moses' mother, taking him by the hand when he was a little boy, walking to the door of her cabin, and pointing her finger to the fields where the Hebrews were toiling and sweating and suffering under the burning sun, beneath the slave-drivers's whip with bruised and bleeding backs, pining and groaning and wishing to die. I can hear her saying, "Moses my child, do you see those slaves? They are your brethren, your people. You belong to them and they belong to you. You have been dedicated to deliver them. God has chosen you to save them some day. Never forget it, Moses. Soon you will leave us to go to school in the king's house, and you will hear much against us, but remember, Moses, what Mother tells you, and when the time comes for you to deliver your people, God will help you." And I can hear the little fellow as he was looking big-eyed over the fields, then looking into the tear-filled eyes of the mother, lisping "No, Mama, I will never forget it. I will always remember and do what God wants me to do."

OFF TO SCHOOL

Then Moses went off to school, college and the university, but he never got away from mother's teaching those first few years, and forty years later it came into his heart to visit his brethren and to announce to them that God "by his hand would deliver them." They rejected him and Moses went to the backside of the desert, but even there never got away from mother's prayers and mother's instruction. Where did Moses get his information? From Mother and Father. Here lies the lesson today.

We read with alarm the staggering statistics of the increase of crime among the youth and the lowering of the age of juvenile delinquency and call it by its right name, *parental delinquency*. The first few years, while children are still in the home, are the important years. Fortify them there, put God's Word under their feet there and you need not worry when they enter high school, college and the university. The Jesuit fathers are quoted as saying, "Give us the child until he is seven, and you may have him the rest of its life." No truer thing could ever be said.

THE CAUSE OF DELINQUENCY

Here, then, is the cause of the delinquency problem, *the home*. All of the well-meaning efforts by all the agencies in the world will never, never check the rising tide of juvenile crime and delinquency until we attack this evil at its source. With almost one out of every three marriages ending in divorce and a broken home, with women who have assumed the responsibility of motherhood spending their time in social life and entrusting the care of their children to outsiders, with mothers who ought to know better spending their time in taverns and amusement places, sipping cocktails and playing cards, with the fathers playing golf and spending their nights at their clubs and lodges when they should be home doing the biggest job in all the world, fortifying their children for the coming temptations of life, we are not surprised at the awful increase in wickedness and crime.

I call upon you fathers and mothers who still have some sense of responsibility of parenthood left, to *stop, stop* right where you are and ask yourself, "Have I a right to bring children into the world without dedicating my life to the proper care and training of those who come into the world by no choice of their own, but wholly by the choice of those whose duty it is to give, not a good, not a better, but the *best* of Christian training during the earliest and most important years of life?"

I plead with you, will you dedicate yourself today to this important task? All other sincere and earnest efforts must and will fail until we begin at the source, the home. No home can be the best home in which to rear children until it is a Christian home. Only Christ can make you the parent you ought to be. Begin, therefore, first of all, by receiving Christ as your Saviour and then lead your children to Christ. God has promised, as he proved in the case of Moses, "Train up a child in the way that he should go: and when he is old, he will not depart from it" (Proverbs 22:6).

Chapter Fourteen

Take Off Your Shoes

> Now Moses kept the flock of Jethro his father in law, the
> . . . and he led the flock to the backside of the desert
> . . . (Exodus 3:1).

It is a sad fact that men never backslide alone. They
are not content to gripe alone, but always seek to lead
others astray as well. It was ever thus. We have already
pointed out the fact that Moses was not in the place of
service which befitted his preparation and calling when he
fled, in disgust at the ingratitude of the Hebrews whom he
had tried to help, to the backside of the desert. No, he had
to lead the *flock* there too. Sad indeed that even the flock
is led astray by the leaders who are out of the will of
God. Such is the nature of sin and disobedience. Thank
God that He does not forget His backsliding child, like
the backsliding believer tries to forget God, but He follows
him, and sooner or later will deal with him.

Moses, we have pointed out repeatedly, *knew* what God's
will for his life was. He knew he was called to deliver
these Hebrew children, but instead of biding God's time, he
chose his own time, only to be rejected and to flee in dismay. In a former chapter we tried to show that this
knowledge of his mission Moses must have learned at his
mother's knee when in those few early years in his father's
house, before he went for his schooling in the institutions
at the court of Pharaoh, he had been so perfectly taught

and indoctrinated by his parents that he was never able to get away from that influence. There is nothing which can take the place of a Christian training in the home during the earliest tender years of a child's life. If this is neglected you may send them later to all of the fine Christian institutions in the world, but you can never undo the damage your neglect in those early years has done. All the Christian schools, Christian colleges and academies, cannot substitute for home training. The job of a Christian father and mother in raising a family for God is the biggest business in the world, and the one that is taken more lightly and neglected more than any other.

I take off my hat to, and praise God every day, for the few Christian mothers in this land who know that training their children for Christ is still the greatest job in the world: greater than to be a special leader, greater than being a career woman, greater than being a civic leader, greater than being president if that were possible for a woman, greater than being a missionary to foreign fields, greater than being a Christian worker among *other* people's children. No one can substitute for you, mother. *No one.* You are the most important person in all the world *in your family.* It may not have the glamor, and gain public recognition like other pursuits, but in the directory of heaven, Godly mothers head the list above philanthropists, preachers, teachers, and the other luminaries in the various fields of service. Your reward will be great, and you can afford to wait for it.

I thank God for the memory of just that kind of a mother now in glory. She never had her name in the paper except when it carried her funeral and death notice. She never attained heights in the public eye, she was just a plain, obscure, Godly, Christian mother who was responsible for everything God has ever been willing to do through me, her son. Whatever rewards I receive when I meet Jesus for any service I have rendered as a preacher and Bible teacher I shall humbly lay at the feet of a little gray-haired mother who knew how to pray and knew how to claim her children for Christ. And I thank God the mother of my children is just like that. God bless her and keep her.

Oh, Christian mothers, do not murmur when you see others doing what you feel are the big and the prominent things and the things which men notice. Yours is still the biggest job: let nothing interfere with your doing it well. The things I learned in the church school, Sunday school and catechism, many, many of them have been forgotten, but what I learned at mother's knee I shall never forget.

BACK TO MOSES AGAIN

We have digressed somewhat from the theme of our message, but we felt that a word in this connection might be both helpful and comforting to some of you weary mothers. I would like to say much more, but we must get back to our visit with Moses on the backside of the desert.

For forty years he is there tending a flock of a few sheep when he should have been helping a dying nation of two million souls. God's time finally came, which Moses in his zeal had wrongly anticipated by forty years. At the end of these years we read,

> And the Angel of the Lord appeared unto him in a flame of fire out of the midst of a bush: and he looked, and behold, the bush burned with fire, and the bush was not consumed.
>
> And Moses said, I will now turn aside, and see this great sight, why the bush is not burnt.
>
> And when the Lord saw that he turned aside to see, God called unto him out of the midst of the bush, and said, Moses, Moses. And he said, Here am I.
>
> And he said, Draw not nigh hither: put off thy shoes from off thy feet, for the place whereon thou standest is holy ground.
>
> Moreover he said, I am the God of thy father, the God of Abraham, the God of Isaac, and the God of Jacob.

And Moses hid his face; for he was afraid to look upon God. (Exodus 3:2-6)

How condescendingly gracious of the Lord to seek after Moses. Moses had no desire to meet God and to go back to Egypt. This is clear from Exodus 2:21: "And Moses was content to dwell with the man . . . " (Jethro in the desert).

How sad when a believer is *content* in his backslidden condition. God is going to have His way anyway and He is going to do what He has promised. And so the Lord sends the *angel of the Lord* (who is always the Lord Jesus in the Old Testament) to rebuke Moses, and bring him back to the place of service. He does it by showing Moses a *burning bush* which burned and burned but was not consumed. The meaning of the burning bush is clear from the context. The bush is the nation of Israel, the poor Hebrews whom Moses had forsaken groveling in slavery in Egypt. God comes and says, "Moses, just because you have forsaken my people, because you felt they were unworthy (and they certainly are) is no reason why I am going to break my covenant with them, the covenant of grace which depends not upon their worthiness but upon *My faithfulness*. Moses, you have tried to wash your hands of this nation and say, God is all through with Israel, He is not going to bring them into their land, but Moses, you are mistaken. *I must keep My word.* I must be faithful to my covenant, no matter how unfaithful *they* are, and how much of a case you can raise against their *right* to be delivered." That God meant to tell Moses this is evident from the narrative:

> And God heard their groaning, and God remembered his covenant with Abraham, with Isaac, and with Jacob.
> And God looked upon the children of Israel, and God had respect unto them (Exodus 2:24-25).

Remembering His covenant He comes to Moses to rebuke him for having forgotten this, and shows him the *burning bush*. This bush is Israel in Egypt, in the fires of persecution and slavery and bondage. The death sentence is passed upon them. All the male babies must be killed and so exterminate in the nation a generation. But the death sentence had failed. The bush was indeed afire, but it was not consumed. The reason is immediately stated. *The angel of the Lord was in the midst of the bush.* God was preserving the Israelites, and keeping them. God saw to it that they were not consumed. This is the lesson of the burning bush which Moses had to learn. The lesson is true today. God has promised to bring this same nation once again into the land of Canaan, never to be plucked up again. Millions of Christians like Moses do not believe it, but God's Word stands and it cannot fail. Again God reveals Himself in that burning bush. After millenniums out of their land, scattered among the nations, burning, persecuted, hated and reviled, the Jews are not consumed because Jehovah God is preserving them till that day when their Great Emancipator, the Lord Jesus, of whom Moses was the type, will come to lead them once more out of bondage into the land of plenty and peace. That is why the nation cannot be destroyed by a Nebuchadnezzar, or an Alexander, a Caesar, a Haman, a Hitler, or a Mussolini. The Jews are the burning bush never to be consumed, but some day to be the fruitful tree of the Lord. This is the lesson Moses needed to learn, and many still need to learn the same lesson.

How God Taught Moses

Patiently the Lord teaches Moses this lesson. First the burning bush, "Do you see it Moses, *burning, burning?* That is My people whom you have forsaken, but I have not. I am still in the midst of them to deliver them. Even though they are unfaithful and have rejected you, My servant, I have not forsaken them for My covenant's sake." How clear the Lord makes this to Moses. Notice the record,

> And the Lord said, I have surely seen the affliction of my people which are in Egypt, and have heard their cry by reason of their taskmasters; for I know their sorrows;
>
> And I am come down to deliver them out of the hand of the Egyptians . . . (Exodus 3:7-8).

What a rebuke for Moses. He thought that because his people were unfaithful God would cast them off, but not so. God will never break his covenant of grace, neither then nor now. Having shown Moses the burning bush, and its significance as representing the nation he had forsaken, the Lord says to Moses: ". . . Draw not nigh higher: put off thy shoes from off thy feet . . . " (Exodus 3:5).

Take your shoes off Moses, and learn your lesson. Why did he have to remove his shoes? Someone has said, because Moses had cold feet when he deserted Israel. However there is a Scriptural reason.

Part of the law of Israel had to do with redeeming a brother, and if a man failed to do his duty by his brethren he was disgraced. As a token of this disgrace his shoe was taken off as a sign that he failed to do his duty toward his brother. The Holy Spirit caused Moses to write down this instruction himself in Deuteronomy:

> If brethren dwell together, and one of them die, and have no child, the wife of the dead shall not marry without unto a stranger: her husband's brother shall . . . take her to him to wife, and perform the duty of a husband's brother unto her.
>
> And if the man like not to take his brother's wife, then let his brother's wife go . . . unto the elders, and say, My husband's brother . . . will not perform the duty of my husband's brother.
>
> Then the elders of the city shall call him, and speak unto him: and if he stand to it, and say, I like not to take her;
>
> Then shall his brother's wife come unto him . . . and loose his shoe from off his foot, and spit in his face, and shall answer and say, So shall it be done unto that man that will not build up his brother's house.
>
> And his name shall be called in Israel, The house of him that hath his shoe loosed. (Deuteronomy 25:5, 7, 8-10)

The teaching is plain. It was a law that if a man died without a child, then if possible the deceased man's brother was to take the wife as a duty to redeem the name of his brother. If he failed in this duty to his brother, he was disgraced and as a symbol of that disgrace, his shoe was removed from his foot.

I trust you will see why God said to Moses take off thy shoes from off thy feet. His brethren were suffering in Egypt while he, their redeemer, was on the backside of the desert. Off with your shoes Moses and get back into the place where God wants you, back to Egypt and your suffering brethren. Do your duty. Do your duty, Moses. Is it any wonder that after this rebuke, we read: "Moses hid his face; for he was afraid to look upon God" (Exodus 3:6b).

Ah, my friend, are you too on the backside of the desert? You were once active and on fire for God. Then something happened. The very ones to whom you ministered and did the most for, turned on you like the Israelites on Moses. You had a bitter experience in the church and received some very unchristian treatment from those who called themselves Christians. So you ran away to the backside of the desert and quit serving the Lord. You are discouraged and disgusted with people who have not appreciated your service and sacrifice. Why take it out on the Lord? If God will put up with those blundering children of His because of His grace and His covenant, who are you to judge them and run away? Come here and let Him restore you to joy and fellowship.

Are you the one who today has become bitter and cold and cynical because of the inconsistencies of other Christians, and are you on the backside of the desert? I have been trying to loosen your shoe for you, that you may return to the place of service and joy. Will you let God talk to you, will you confess that you have lost your joy and power and turn to Him now and let Him restore you and recommission you to go forward, looking only to Jesus and from this day on taking your eyes *off men* and their failures but seeing *only Jesus?*

Maybe you were a preacher or teacher or Sunday school worker or personal worker or officer in the church. You were so active once, but today are on the backside of the desert, burying your talent in the earth. Oh, humble yourself now and confess it all to Him. Learn the lesson of the burning bush, take off your shoes and let Him wash your feet for service again as Jesus did His disciples. "If we confess our sins, he is faithful and just to forgive us our sins, and to cleanse us from all unrighteousness" (I John 1:9).

Chapter Fifteen

THE WAY BACK HOME

THE MAN MOSES WAS A PRINCE of Egypt and a servant of the Lord, called to lead the Hebrew children out of bondage and into the promised land. Because of a great disappointment in his life, he was out of the place of duty and herding a little flock of sheep on the backside of the desert as far away from those miserable ingrates in Egypt as he could possibly go. No servant of the Lord ever gets so far away that God cannot find him. After forty years of fruitless backsliding, God visits Moses in the burning bush. The bush represents Israel whom Moses had deserted, always in the fire, but miraculously preserved by the presence of a covenant keeping God. God shows Moses his mistake by ordering him to take the shoes off his feet, the symbol of disgrace for having failed to do his duty by his brethren.

Taking off the shoe was a testimony of failure to redeem a brother's lost inheritance as we have seen in a previous Chapter. Now Moses had failed his people and to emphasize this God says, Moses, take off your shoes. The shoe is removed, Moses is rebuked, and now God begins to show Moses how he must go back to the place from whence he had fled and deliver Israel according to God's original plan and purpose.

Read the balance of Exodus 3 and all of chapter 4 to see the patience of God's tender dealing with his returning servant. He pleads with him, and in spite of all of Moses' many, many objections, continues to bear with him until at last Moses does arise and starts back to the land of Egypt, his despised brethren and the place of duty.

It is not easy to retrace one's steps from the backside of the desert. Pride stands in the way. How difficult it is for the backslider to admit his wrong and come in humble repentance to the Lord. But it must be done or the most terrible results will follow when the Lord lays His hand of chastening upon him. The backslider must return. If he does so obediently and willingly, God graciously forgives and restores. If he refuses to come back willingly, God has another and far more unpleasant method to accomplish His purpose anyway. It is a dangerous thing for a believer to be out of fellowship with God. Every moment he spends in that condition he is inviting the chastening and judgment of God.

THE SIN UNTO DEATH

It was so in the case of Moses. After all God's pleading, Moses still does not come willingly, and so God seeks to kill him rather than let him continue in his stubbornness. Yes, I said God sought to kill Moses and take him home to be cleansed at the judgment seat of Christ rather than let him go on in disobedience. We have this record written afterwards by Moses himself in Exodus 4:24. The Lord is angry with Moses (Exodus 4:14) and then we read:

> And it came to pass by the way in the inn, that the Lord met him, and sought to kill him.
>
> Then Zipporah took a sharp stone, and cut off the foreskin of her son, and cast it at his feet, and said, Surely a bloody husband art thou to me.
>
> So he let him go: then she said, A bloody husband thou art, because of the circumcision (Exodus 4:24-26).

God met the grumbling Moses, his servant and child, and sought to kill him. God will not leave his erring child go on in rebellion. Either he must repent or God will visit him with affliction and even, if it becomes necessary, will slay him. God wants His people clean. He will not tolerate continued sinning. He must and will take a hand, and if the child of God continues in unrepentance, the Lord may have to take him out by the way of death rather than let him go on.

This is not only true in the case of Moses, but also is taught in the New Testament. In I Corinthians 11, Paul is speaking of coming to the Lord's table, the place of most intimate fellowship with the Lord and the brethren. The Christian is to examine his own heart, confess all his sin, and then only can he be blessed of the Lord. To refuse this is to invoke the judgment of God. Listen to Paul:

> But let a man examine himself, and so let him eat of that bread, and drink of that cup.
>
> For he that eateth and drinketh unworthily, eateth and drinketh damnation (Judgment) to himself, not discerning the Lord's body.
>
> For this cause many are weak and sickly among you, and many sleep.
>
> For if we would judge ourselves, we should not be judged (I Cor. 11:28-31).

The teaching of this passage is not only crystal clear, but is tremendously important. God plainly says that because these Corinthian believers would not judge sin in their own lives, but continued without confessing it, that many of them were weak, others were sick, and many were dead. Paul distinctly says "many sleep." Oh, how important this truth, for simple, humble confession of sin would cure many ills of God's people. There are afflictions and weaknesses and sicknesses for which there is no medicine and which no doctor can help until the believer is willing to confess and forsake his sin. Whom the Lord loveth, He chasteneth, and scourgeth every son whom he receiveth. God will not answer our prayer for healing until we have judged ourselves first. Let me repeat, God wants His people clean.

Let me add that not all weakness and sickness among believers is because of unconfessed sin. I dare say only a comparatively few are weak because of this, but the fact remains just the same that many of God's children are suffering because of unconfessed sin, and if continued in, there is only one thing for God to do, take that child home by death to be cleansed at the judgment seat of Christ. Remember, therefore, that continued sinning against better light brings the chastening and judgment of the Lord.

THE CASE OF MOSES

For the above reason, then, the Lord met Moses and sought to kill him, and only one thing saved him. Zipporah, Moses' wife, took a sharp stone and circumcised their son, and that averted the judgment of God upon Moses. Circumcision of all male sons was the commandment of God, given way back in the days of Abraham. It was God's mark upon His people of His covenant relationship with Israel. It identified them as the people of God with whom he had made an unconditional and unbreakable covenant of grace. Moses had neglected to administer this rite of circumcision to his own son. The reason is obvious.

Since the rite of circumcision identified one as belonging to the nation of Israel, and Moses was so disappointed with that nation that he virtually disowned them, he refused to be identified with them by preventing his own son from having the mark of identification with these Hebrews who had so shamefully rejected him. Moses seems to say by his refusal to give this sign to his own son, "I will have nothing to do with this nation. I would not even have my son identified with them." But God, who always keeps His covenant, was still in the midst of the burning bush of

Israel. Though disobedient, the Israelites were still His people.

THE MEANING OF THE RITE

This was the occasion for Moses' repentance and the appeasing of the wrath of God against him. God stayed His hand when He saw this act of Zipporah. Now, whatever various groups of Christians may think of Old Testament circumcision, all are agreed, I am sure, as to the spiritual meaning. It represents the cutting away of the filth of the flesh. It was a painful operation, but essential for blessing. It was a bloody operation, but indispensable to receive the favor of God. Moses had refused, but before blessing can come, this painful and bloody process must be performed.

There was only one way for Moses to leave behind the backside of the desert and his job of shepherding his little flock, and that was through this rite, symbolizing that he was now cutting away forever, no matter how painful it might be, all confidence in the flesh, all the filth of his own sinful rebellion and sinful stubbornness.

The application for us is simple. While this literal rite and ceremony ceased with Calvary and has no application to the body of Christ as an obligation, the spiritual lesson is nevertheless clear. If we are to examine ourselves and live in fellowship with the Lord and bring forth the maximum of service to Him, we too must be willing to cut away all filthiness of the flesh, put away all known and doubtful sin, judge every sin in our lives, and come to Him in absolute surrender and contrition. There is no other way. If pride keeps us from doing this, then sooner or later, the Lord Himself will have to take a hand. I assure you that when He deals with you, it will be far more unpleasant and painful than if you willingly confess your sin and seek forgiveness.

In concluding these chapters on the backside of the desert, I want to end on a very definitely practical note. The purpose of bringing these messages is to get those of you who are on the backside of the desert to see the simple way back into the joy, fellowship and service of the Lord. I know there are thousands who once knew the joy of serving the Lord, teachers, personal workers, preachers, and others, who were happy and being used of God, but who today are on the backside of the desert. While you may put on a bold front to save face, and let your pride keep you from admitting how miserable you really are, God knows your heart. He loves you, He wants to draw you back again. He has said to you. "Put off thy shoes from off thy feet." Will you right now take the knife of His Word, the sword of the Spirit, and by humble confession and repentance of your condition cut away all which is hindering your spiritual life and grieving your Lord?

Let me add this word of warning. If you will not, then remember God loves you too much to let you alone. Sooner or later He will take a hand and may bring upon you His chastening in weakness, in sickness, and even death. That is, *if* you are His child. If you are not really His child, He will probably let you go on, but if you belong to Him, He *will* have you clean.

What is it in your life which stands between you and victory? Some habit? Some sin? A bitter spirit? An unforgiving, stubborn will? Worldly pleasure? Lack of prayer? Gossip, bitterness? What is it, my friend? Come now and confess it to Him and move from the lonely, miserable backside of the desert into the place of blessing, service, joy and reward. What a glorious record of Moses' achievements follows the last cutting away of Moses' pride and wilfulness. From here on Moses goes to Egypt, defies the king, works great miracles, leads out two million slaves for forty years to the land of promise. His name has gone down in history as the greatest of all Old Testament characters, and the great emancipator of the chosen nation. God, too, has something great and wonderful for you if you will return to Him for, "If we confess our sins he is faithful and just to forgive us our sins, and to cleanse us from all unrighteousness" (I John 1:9).

Chapter Sixteen

GOD'S LONG RANGE PROGRAM

WE ARE LIVING IN AN AGE of complicated programs and long-range planning. We have heard a great deal about the Five Year Plan, the Ten Year Plan, and only recently Hitler's One Hundred Year Plan for world peace and prosperity. Agencies have multiplied like dandelions in the past few years as part of our own long-range planning in crop insurance, social reform, defense programs, soil conservation, flood control, health insurance, social security, reforestation and long-range recovery programs. We have almost exhausted the alphabet in designating the innumerable agencies created to carry out this long-range social, economic and security program.

All of this activity, however, only reflects the unending search of man for an age of security and the realization of the four or more freedoms of which man has been dreaming. None of man's programs are perfect, and in spite of all man's efforts, floods continue, famine still stalks, crops still fail, poverty continues, and the threat of war hangs darker than ever. Never before have we been more conscious of our own insecurity. So we look away from the fallible program of man to another long-range plan, conceived in the heart of Almighty God thousands of years ago, and revealed in His Holy Book, the Bible. This program of God is the One Thousand Year Plan, God's long-range program of security, prosperity and peace.

The Bible predicts that at the end of the ages, there will be an era of one thousand years of peace and prosperity and plenty, when wars will be utterly unknown, all manufacture of weapons will cease, famines and want be banished, sickness conquered, poverty abolished, flood, storms and hunger be forever gone, and all the world will be one great united nation under the government of one King, the Lord Jesus Christ Himself.

This golden age is called in the Bible the Millennium, and the Kingdom. In the following chapters we shall try to give you a broad outline of this coming age of peace. The Bible abounds with information concerning this blessed day, so we can only give you the high points of Scripture revelation, and trust that it will stimulate you to study it more thoroughly for yourself.

We begin this introductory chapter by referring first of all to the last book in the Bible, the book of Revelation, chapter twenty verses 4-6:

> And I saw thrones, and they sat upon them, and judgment was given unto them: and I saw the souls of them that were beheaded for the witness of Jesus, and for the word of God, and which had not worshipped the beast, neither his image, neither had received his mark upon their foreheads, or in their hands; and they lived and reigned with Christ a thousand years.
>
> But the rest of the dead lived not again until the thousand years were finished. This is the first resurrection.
>
> Blessed and holy is he that hath part in the first resurrection: on such the second death hath no power, but they shall be priests of God and of Christ, and shall reign with him a thousand years (Revelation 20:4-6).

In this passage the expression, "one thousand years," is used three times. In all it is mentioned six times in this chapter alone. This thousand years is usually referred to as the Millennium, or the Kingdom, here mentioned as one thousand years, but fully described throughout the Bible both in the Old and the New Testaments. Before taking up some of the many, many Scripture passages dealing with this coming age, we wish first to define the word. Often we hear someone objecting that the word *millennium* does not occur in the Bible. This is a result of misunderstanding of the word. In the passage which we read, the expression, a thousand years, is used six times in this chapter alone. Now the word in the Greek is "chiliad," meaning one thousand years. The word *millennium* itself, is the Latin equivalent of "a thousand years." The word comes from two other words, "mille" meaning one thousand, and the word, "annus" meaning years, so that the expression *millennium* is merely the Latin phrase for our English equivalent, one thousand years.

THE BIBLE DOCTRINE

The Bible doctrine concerning the millennium is that there will be a period of exactly one thousand years during which Jesus Christ will reign on this earth together with His church. During this millennium, following immediately the Second Coming of the Lord Jesus, Israel as a Nation will be re-established in the land of Palestine. The nations will be at peace. There will be no war, no preparations for war, no military training, no armies, no navies, and no military air forces of any kind. Peace and prosperity will reign throughout the earth. The Lord Jesus Himself will be the only King, and the only Ruler, and for this one thousand years the problems of humanity will be completely solved.

Belief in the coming millennial age dates from the very beginning of the history of the nation of Israel. In the International Standard Bible Encyclopedia, we read this statement:

> The doctrine of a temporary Messianic Kingdom preceding the consumation of the world's history is of pre-Christian Jewish origin.

Another quotation from the same encyclopedia reads as follows:

The great majority of evangelical-Christians believe that the Kingdom of God shall have universal sway over the earth and that righteousness and peace and the knowledge of the Lord shall everywhere prevail. This happy time is commonly called the Millennium, or the One Thousand Years' Reign. Divergent views are entertained as to how it is to be brought about. Many honest and faithful men hold that it will be introduced by the agencies now at work, mainly by the preaching of the gospel of Christ and the extension of the Church over the world. However, an increasing number of men, equally honest, teach that the millennium will be established by the visible advent of the Lord Jesus Christ.

I have given these two quotations because one of them is by an avowed postmillennialist, and the other by one who accepts and embraces the premillennial teaching.

THREE SCHOOLS OF INTERPRETATION

With regard to this golden age of peace and prosperity upon the earth, there are at least three main interpretations. First of all, we have the premillennial interpretation from the word, "pre," which means before, and "millennium" which means a thousand years. In brief, the premillennial interpretation teaches that this golden age will be ushered in by the personal return of the Lord. This is the reason it is called "premillennial," because it teaches that Christ will return to the earth before the establishment of the Kingdom upon the earth.

Second, we have the postmillennial interpretation, which teaches that the Lord Jesus will not return until *after* the millennial age. In brief, the postmillennial theory teaches that the world will become gradually better and better. Men, as the result of education, reformation, religious teaching, understanding, conferences and law, will finally succeed in abolishing war, in bringing about an age of peace, and the whole world will become converted to Christendom. Then the thousand years of peace will follow, and the coming again of Christ at the end of the world to judge all men. As we shall have occasion to show, we believe this interpretation to be in conflict both with the clear teaching of the Word of God and the facts of human history. One has but to look round about him today and see that the world is not getting better, but is rapidly declining in morals and increasing in violence and crime and in wickedness, in harmony with the prophetic Word.

There is a third interpretation of more recent origin, which is called the a-millennial, which as the word implies, means no millennium at all. The prefix "a", is a negative prefix, and means simply, "no millennium." It is a flat denial of the literal reign of the Lord Jesus upon this earth, either before or after His second coming. A-millennialists, therefore, spiritualize all of the prophecies which refer to this coming kingdom age.

PREMILLENNIALISM IS AS OLD AS THE BIBLE

It may be well at this point to remind you that the premillennial teaching has been held by the church of Jesus Christ from the very beginning. As we said before, it began even before the first advent of Christ. This golden kingdom age was the hope of the Old Testament Israelite who looked forward to the coming of the Messiah, and at the coming of the Messiah the establishment of a Messianic Kingdom upon the earth. This was the hope of the disciples and John the Baptist and all the orthodox Jews in Jesus' day. It is still the hope of multitudes of orthodox Jews throughout the world at this very time. They are still looking for and expecting the coming of their Messiah who will re-establish them in their own land and bring about the Messianic Kingdom of peace and of righteousness. There is nothing in the Word of God, however, to indicate that this peace will come before the return of the Messiah, and so the premillennial interpretation is not only the Scriptural one, we believe, but the oldest one by centuries.

The postmillennial explanation was not advanced until

centuries after the establishment of the church, and was advanced first merely as a theory. The one who advanced it had no idea whatsoever that it would be accepted as a doctrine which could be defended or supported. The theory was adopted by those who refused to accept the literal interpretation of Scripture.

The a-millennial interpretation is of even more recent origin. A-millennialism is disillusioned postmillennialism. Postmillennialism, with its doctrine of the world gettng better and better, received a very rude shock during the past generation, with its two global wars, and with the increase of wickedness and crime. So the honest postmillennarian was forced to admit that the world was not getting better, and if the millennium was to be ushered in by the efforts of man, it was farther away from that goal now than it had ever been before. Rather than admitting that the premillennial view was the correct one, they adopted a theory of a-millennialism, which is a denial of the literal reign of Christ upon the earth, according to their interpretation.

In this chapter it is our main purpose, therefore, to show that this millennial age of peace and righteousness, this one thousand years of blessing upon the literal earth, will come after the return of our precious Lord, and that the entire body of Scripture is in harmony with this fact, and that it can only be ushered in by His imminent return.

MUCH CONFUSION OF PROGRAM

Before taking up the details of this millennial age, we would like to give you a brief outline of the order of events as revealed in Scripture, and then in our next chapter go into the detail of that which the Bible foretells concerning the blessings of this golden age. A great deal of confusion exists in the minds of God's people in regard to the exact pattern of future events as given in the Word. This is due partly to the fact that Christians do not always study their Bibles as they should, and partly due to the fact that many have lost interest because of the diversity of opinion which exists among those who do study the Bible.

Now for the order of events. We believe the next event in the program of God will be the coming of Christ for His Church, usually called the Rapture. When Christ comes He will appear in the sky, He will shout from the air, and all believers who are asleep in Christ will arise in resurrection bodies, all living believers will be instantaneously changed and they together will be caught up to meet the Lord in the air. Then will follow a period of seven years called the Tribulation period, during which God will judge the nations of the earth, and the Church will be prepared for the wedding of the Lamb at the judgment seat of Christ. At the close of this seven years the Lord Jesus Himself will return visibly and publicly with His church to this earth, He will destroy His enemies, will re-gather the nation of Israel into the land, the land of Palestine, and will usher in the millennial age of peace when Satan shall be bound for a thousand years. So we do believe with all our hearts that the next event on the program of God is the return of Christ for the Church, to take us unto Himself, and then to pour judgment upon this earth and to cleanse it from all His adversaries.

In the following chapters we shall bring some of the details of the Bible teaching concerning this event, but before we go into detail, it is necessary that we have a clear picture of the events as they will develop.

At the close of the millennial age Satan will be loosed for a short season to prove the incorrigibility, not only of Satan, but also of unregenerate human nature. He will be destroyed and cast into the lake of fire together with all his followers, and then the earth will be purified by fire, and a new heaven and a new earth will be created by God which shall be the dwelling place of the redeemed throughout all the ages. This is God's long-range plan. This is God's program for this earth. The Bible has so much to say about this and it is so clear in its teachings it behooves all of us to study His Word and study God's plan that we may know what He is doing and be ready for His appearing.

Chapter Seventeen

CREATION RESTORED

The wilderness and the solitary place shall be glad for them; and the desert shall rejoice, and blossom as the rose.

And the parched ground shall become a pool, and the thirsty land springs of water (Isaiah 35:1, 7).

Every valley shall be exalted and every mountain and hill shall be made low: and the crooked shall be made straight, and the rough places plain.

And the glory of the Lord shall be revealed, and all flesh shall see it together: for the mouth of the Lord hath spoken it (Isaiah 40:4-5).

And the Lord shall be King over all the earth: in that day shall there be one Lord, and his name one.

All the land shall be turned as a plain from Geba to Rimmon south of Jerusalem: and it shall be lifted up, and inhabited in her place . . . (Zechariah 14:9-10).

THESE ARE BUT A FEW of the many passages throughout the entire Word of God which we might quote from prophecy indicating the glorious day which the Lord has promised in His Word which will come at the return of the Lord Jesus Christ. As we have pointed out in the previous chapter, the Bible clearly predicts that there is a coming golden age in the future when the Lord Jesus Christ will personally reign upon this earth, and all the world will be at peace. When He comes again at the close of the tribulation and destroys the armies at Armageddon, the earth and all the creation will undergo physical changes unknown before in the history of mankind.

COMPLETE REDEMPTION

It is well to remember that when Adam, our first parent, sinned, he did not sin as an individual, and when he fell he fell not alone, but he fell as the representative, federal head of God's entire earthly creation. In Adam was represented not only the whole race, that is, the human race which would spring from him, but Adam was also the federal head and the representative of all that God had created on this earth, and over which Adam had received dominion. So when our first parents sinned, the curse of God not only fell on them, and on his human descendants, but upon the entire world, and it all came under the curse. The mineral kingdom, the vegetable kingdom, the animal kingdom, all came unwillingly under the curse of Adam's sin, because of this headship and relationship. Here is the Word of God, as He comes to curse the earth because of Adam's sin:

> Cursed is the ground for thy sake; in sorrow shalt thou eat of it all the days of thy life;
> Thorns also and thistles shall it bring forth to thee; and thou shalt eat the herb of the field;
> In the sweat of thy face shalt thou eat bread, till thou return unto the ground; for out of it wast thou taken: for dust thou art, and unto dust shalt thou return (Genesis 3:17-19).

Notice that God cursed the ground for Adam's sake. Because of Adam's sin, even the mineral creation came under the curse of God. Before sin came, the ground was perfect and one hundred per cent productive. God never made a desert, God never made bad lands or waste lands, for when He had created all things, He saw all things He had made, and behold, it was very good. Then sin entered, the curse fell, deserts appeared, and today, instead of the earth willingly producing her wealth, man must wrest its stores from her by constant sweat and toil while the whole creation, according to Paul in

Romans eight, "groaneth and travaileth in pain together until now."

The Vegetable Realm

Just as the earth, the soil itself, came under Adam's curse, so too we are told that the vegetation came under the curse of God, for He said, "Thorns also and thistles shall it bring forth to thee."

Weeds, insects, pests and plant disease came because of sin, and the creation became restricted in its productivity and sharply limited in its ability to bring forth the needs of man. Look at the struggle which we have in nature today. What toiling and sweating as the farmer fights for his crops against the disease and the pests and the weeds which make the uninterrupted battle of God's creation against the results of sin. Man calls it the struggle for existence, and the survival of the fittest, but God says it is the curse of sin which rests on all the earth because of Adam's trangression.

The Animal Creation

From the mineral through the vegetable, the curse reached on through even to the animal, and God goes on to say to the serpent, then the most beautiful of all animal creation, and probably standing at the head of the beast creation: "Thou art cursed above all cattle, and above every beast of the field; upon thy belly shalt thou go, and dust shalt thou eat all the days of thy life" (Genesis 3:14).

All the animals were cursed by Adam's sin, but the serpent was cursed above them all because he had been the instrument for the introduction of sin and of this curse. Before the fall there were no carnivorous animals. Adam was a vegetarian. There is no record in the Bible of man's ever eating meat until after the flood. All the animals were docile and harmless. There was no preying the one upon the other, but all was peace and quiet and happiness among God's creation. Sin then entered, and changed the nature of God's whole handiwork: animals, birds and fish suddenly found their appetites perverted and began preying one upon the other until truly we can say, "The whole creation groaneth and travaileth in pain together until now." Man calls it the struggle for existence and the survival of the fittest, but God says it is creation crying for redemption.

THE LAST ADAM

As the first Adam brought the curse through sin, so the last Adam, the Lord Jesus Christ, came to make payment for sin and to remove the very curse which lay upon creation because of Adam's transgression. In order to be a complete redeemer, His redemption must reach into every realm which Adam lost. Since Adam dragged all and every realm of creation with him under the curse, the vegetable, the mineral and the animal, Jesus Christ, to be a perfect Redeemer, must also redeem all of these realms which Adam lost. We usually think of Christ's redemptive work as being limited only to fallen mankind, but it is just as true that Jesus died on the cross of Calvary to redeem the soil and the plants and the beasts and the birds and the fish from the curse which came unwillingly upon them. It may at first seem that this belittles the work of Christ, that He should not only die for men, but when one thinks it through, it really exalts His redemptive work, for He is a complete redeemer. God never made anything waste. God never made a desert.

The condition in which we find the earth in the first part of Genesis was the result of a curse which lay upon the earth because of the sin of the fallen angels before the creation of man. After God had restored the earth and placed man upon it, sin again entered and the curse again fell upon the entire creation. Since sin made the earth barren to a large extent, we believe that when Jesus comes He will make the earth once more like the

Garden of Eden. The Bible is clear on this matter. In Isaiah 35:1 we read: "The wilderness and the solitary place shall be glad for them; and the desert shall rejoice, and blossom as the rose."

The context of this entire passage shows that the prophet is speaking of that glorious golden millennial age when the Lord Jesus Christ shall come to restore that which was placed under the curse because of the sin of mankind. In Ezekiel thirty-four we read the following description of that wonderful, golden age:

> And I will make them and the places round about my hill a blessing; and I will cause the shower to come down in his season; there shall be showers of blessing.
>
> And the tree of the field shall yield her fruit, and the earth shall yield her increase, and they shall be safe in their land, and shall know that I am the Lord . . . (Ezekiel 34:26-27).

The prophet Hosea in the second chapter of his prophecy voices the same glad cry as he describes that happy day of Jesus' reign on the earth by saying:

> And in that day (that is, the day when Jesus rules in Jerusalem and the nation of Israel is restored in the land, as the context will show) will I make a covenant for them with the beasts of the field and with the fowls of heaven, and with the creeping things of the ground: and I will break the bow and the sword and the battle out of the earth, and will make them to lie down safely (Hosea 2:18).

NEW TESTAMENT REVELATION

Not only is this the burden of prophecy in the Old Testament, but even after the cross of Calvary we can turn to the New Testament revelation and find the same precious blessed promises concerning this golden age of peace. Many people imagine that the Old Testament only contains prophetic truth, but the New Testament too is full of it, and teaches that the kingdom promises of blessing and peace were not fulfilled at the first coming, for they are repeated again and again after Jesus went to heaven. In the epistle of Paul to the Romans, in the eighth chapter, we have Paul speaking about the redemption of the whole creation at the coming of the Lord Jesus Christ:

> For the earnest expectation of the creation waiteth for the manifestation of the sons of God.
>
> For the creation was made subject to vanity, not willingly, but by reason of him who hath subjected the same in hope,
>
> Because the creation itself also shall be delivered from the bondage of corruption into the glorious liberty of the children of God.
>
> For we know that the whole creation groaneth and travaileth in pain together until now (Romans 8:19-22).

From these verses we notice that the expectation of creation is for the manifestation of the sons of God. Now the manifestation of the sons of God will occur at the close of the tribulation period when we are manifested with Christ at His glorious second coming. During the tribulation period the whole creation will be subjected to a tremendous bath of blood during that terrible time of trial and destruction, and so Paul tells us that the creation, including the vegetable as well as the animal creation, is already sighing and longing for the time when Christ shall come to redeem them from under the curse and to bring about again the glorious and wonderful restoration of conditions as they were before sin entered into the world.

THE ANIMAL CREATION

The Bible not only tells us that the earth will be redeemed as far as the soil is concerned, and vegetation will be redeemed so that the entire world will become again like the Garden of Eden, but even the animal creation will share in this redemption. Isaiah tells us:

> The wolf also shall dwell with the lamb, and the leopard shall lie down with the kid; and the calf and the young lion and the fatling together; and a little child shall lead them.
>
> And the cow and the bear shall feed; their young ones shall lie down together: and the lion shall eat straw like the ox.

> And the sucking child shall play on the hole of the asp, and the weaned child shall put his hand on the cockatrice' den.
>
> They shall not hurt nor destroy in all my holy mountain: for the earth shall be full of the knowledge of the Lord, as the waters cover the sea (Isaiah 11:6-9).

If we simply accept this passage as the clear revelation of the Word of God without attempting to place our own interpretation upon it or to twist it by spiritualizing it or calling it symbolic language, we have no difficulty. It simply means that in that golden age, which the context clearly indicates is the age of Christ's reign upon the earth when Israel will be restored in the land, even the animal creation will be at peace. This promise is reiterated in many passages of the Bible. In Isaiah sixty-five we read:

> The wolf and the lamb shall feed together, and the lion shall eat straw like the bullock: and dust shall be the serpent's meat. They shall not hurt nor destroy in all my holy mountain (Isaiah 65:25).

Or turn to Ezekiel thirty-four:

> And I will make with them a covenant of peace, and will cause the evil beasts to cease out of the land: and they shall dwell safely in the wilderness, and sleep in the woods (Ezekiel 34:25).

What a wonderful time that will be. How our hearts beat with glad anticipation when we think of that glorious age of one thousand years upon the earth with Jesus personally present reigning in Jerusalem, the very place where He was crucified: When Israel, who had rejected Him, will be saved and settled in peace in the land according to their inheritance in the Twelve Tribes, forever blessed and safe from their enemies, and we, the Church, the Bride of Christ, reigning with Him there. The curse will be gone; the earth shall bring forth unrestricted and in unlimited abundance. There will be no storms to destroy, no wars to devastate and kill, no wild animals to tear, but all will be peace under the righteous reign of Him Who said He would come and will not tarry.

Surely as we look round about us upon the struggle which is going on in every realm of creation today, and the deepening clouds of coming judgment rising higher upon the horizon, every Christian's eyes should be lifted toward heaven for that next event when the Lord Jesus Christ shall descend from heaven with a shout to take us unto Himself. How we ought to pray as we have never prayed before:

> Our Father which art in heaven, Hallowed be thy name. Thy Kingdom come. Thy will be done in earth, as it is in heaven.

That prayer which has gone up from the hearts of countless millions of Christians ever since Jesus taught it to His disciples has never yet been realized. His kingdom has not yet come. His will is not yet being done on earth as it is in heaven, but blessed be God forever, we know that one of these days that prayer is going to be answered and fulfilled in every detail. I repeat, it has not yet been done. Is there anyone who can look upon the world today and say that God's will is being done on earth as it is in heaven? Can we look upon our own country with all of its sin and all of its failures and its corruption and immorality and sin, and say this is the kingdom and God's will is being done on earth as it is in heaven? Surely none of us are foolish enough to say that. But there is a time coming when we shall cry, "The kingdom has come." It will be the end of all tribulation when the seventh angel sounds his trumpet. In Revelation 11:15 we read:

> And the seventh angel sounded; and there were great voices in heaven, saying, The kingdoms of this world are become the kingdoms of our Lord, and of his Christ; and he shall reign for ever and ever.

May God haste that glad day, and in the meantime set us on fire to send forth far and wide the message, the vital message so much needed today—Jesus Christ is coming again.

Chapter Eighteen

Israel in the Land

Behold, the day of the Lord cometh, and thy spoil shall be divided in the midst of thee.

For I will gather all nations against Jerusalem to battle; and the city shall be taken, and the houses rifled, and the women ravished; and half of the city shall go forth into captivity, and the residue of the people shall not be cut off from the city.

Then shall the Lord go forth, and fight against those nations, as when he fought in the day of battle.

And his feet shall stand in that day upon the mount of Olives, which is before Jerusalem on the east, and the mount of Olives shall cleave in the midst thereof toward the east and toward the west, and there shall be a very great valley; and half of the mountain shall remove toward the north, and half of it toward the south (Zechariah 14:1-4).

And the Lord shall be king over all the earth: in that day there shall be one Lord, and his name one.

All the land shall be turned as a plain from Geba to Rimmon south of Jerusalem: and it shall be lifted up, and inhabited in her place, from Benjamin's gate unto the place of the first gate, unto the corner gate, and from the tower of Hananeel unto the king's winepresses (Zechariah 14:9-10).

IN THE PRECEDING CHAPTERS on the coming Golden Age of Peace, called in Scripture the Millennium, we have seen some of the high points of this wonderful future day which is so abundantly promised throughout the Scriptures. We have seen from the book of Revelation that the Bible is clear in teaching there is an age of one

thousand years coming, the seventh day of God's great
prophetic week, in which will be realized all the dreams
of mankind for security in domestic, social, national and
international life. Not only will there be full redemption
for the children of God when Jesus returns and we receive
our immortal resurrection bodies, but all of the creation
which God has made which came under the curse because of Adam's sin will be redeemed in that day. Paul
tells us in Romans eight that the whole creation today
is waiting for the coming of the Lord. It is travailing and
groaning in pain together until now. Should we as
believers in the Word of God not also be waiting and
crying for that glorious day which is the only hope for
a world that is steeped in sorrow, trouble and misunderstanding? The Bible says that in that day the trees shall
clap their hands, and all the little hills shall skip like
lambs. Should we not also be happy as we anticipate that
glorious golden age of peace?

We now want to take up especially the effect of the
return of the Lord Jesus Christ upon the land of Palestine,
which has been the scene of so much conflict and so much
horror in all the years of her checkered history. Then we
wish to see what the Bible has to say in regard to the
nation of Israel, out of her land for these many, many
centuries, but which according to the Word of God and
in the program of God will again be restored to the land
never to be plucked up again.

THE LAND OF PALESTINE

According to the Word of God, the greatest changes
in the world at the coming again of the Lord Jesus Christ
will occur in the land of Palestine. This is the land which
God gave to Abraham, Isaac, Jacob and the Twelve
Tribes of Israel, by an everlasting covenant. When God
called Abraham out of the Ur of the Chaldees, He promised
him, in an unconditional covenant of grace, that He would
not only give him a seed which would never perish or

cease to be a nation, but He also gave unto him all the land of Canaan as an everlasting possession to him and to his seed after him. For many, many centuries now Israel and the land have been separated from each other. Because of its sin and disobedience to Almighty God, the hand of the Lord has been heavy upon the nation of Israel in chastening, but He has never abrogated or nullified the covenant which He made with Abraham, Isaac and Jacob. The Bible is replete with passages proving that when the Lord Jesus Christ returns again as the Jews' Messiah, He will forgive their iniquity and cleanse their hearts and restore them again to all the blessing which He has promised in days gone by.

In the passage which we read at the beginning of this chapter, we are told that when the Lord Jesus Christ comes again, He will return to the same identical place from which He ascended, the Mount of Olives, to the east of the city of Jerusalem in Palestine. As His feet touch this Mount of Olives, there will result a tremendous earthquake which will split the Mount of Olives in twain, and cause a great valley to be formed from the Mediterranean Sea, even to the Dead Sea. At the same time this mountain is split and this valley is formed, the low places in the land of Palestine will be raised up according to the promises given by Isaiah and the other prophets, that "every valley shall be exalted, and every mountain and hill shall be made low." As a result of this tremendous earthquake and this great convulsion in the land of Palestine, the waters from the Mediterranean Sea will rush in through the valley made by the splitting of the Mount of Olives at the touch of Jesus' feet, and since the Dead Sea will be raised up, these waters will flow to the ocean. Instead of being dead, the Dead sea will become the scene of unparalleled life and activity and the scource of the greatest productivity which the world has ever seen in any area.

Since the land of Canaan and the seed of Abraham can never be dissociated, we find that at the same time the land undergoes its restoration, the nation of Israel will also be restored to their land. In the tribulation period between the Rapture of the Church and the Second Coming of the Lord Jesus, the Bible reveals that there will be a remnant, a faithful remnant of the nation of Israel, one hundred and forty-four thousand in number, twelve thousand from each one of the Twelve Tribes of Israel, who will be supernaturally preserved as the elect of God, and will pass through the tribulation period in preparation for their abode in the land of Palestine. David will be their king, and the twelve apostles will sit upon twelve thrones judging the Twelve Tribes of Israel. This one hundred and forty-four thousand will become the nucleus for the rejuvenated, restored, and converted nation of Israel who will be the praise and the glory of all the earth. Their abode will be in the land of Palestine which then will be the most beautiful and productive spot in all of the earth. They will go into the kingdom age under the reign of their Messiah, the Lord Jesus Christ. Time would utterly fail us to give all of the Scripture passages in the Bible which substantiate the fact that this golden age which is coming will have its special effect upon this nation which will be brought back again never to be plucked up out of their land.

THE FINAL RESTORATION

And in that day there shall be a root of Jesse, which shall stand for an ensign of the people; to it shall the Gentiles seek: and his rest shall be glorious.

And it shall come to pass in that day, that the Lord shall set his hand again the second time to recover the remnant of his people, which shall be left, from Assyria, and from Egypt, and from Pathros, and from Cush, and from Elam, and from Shinar, and from Hamath, and from the islands of the sea.

And he shall set up an ensign for the nations, and shall assemble the outcasts of Israel, and gather together the dispersed of Judah from the four corners of the earth (Isaiah 11:10-12).

If there were no other passage of Scripture in the entire Bible, this would be sufficient to prove that the time is coming when the Lord will recover and bring back the remnant of His people Israel and Judah from the four corners of the earth. This passage in Isaiah forever silences the argument that all of these prophecies were fulfilled at the first return from the captivity in Babylon after the seventy years of dispersion. Here we are told that the Lord will gather them from all the countries of the earth.

The prophet Jeremiah is even more definite and more detailed in his revelation of this wonderful re-gathering of the nation of Israel:

> For there shall be a day, that the watchmen upon the mount Ephraim shall cry, Arise ye, and let us go up to Zion unto the Lord our God (Jeremiah 31:6).
>
> And I will plant them upon their land, and they shall no more be pulled up out of their land which I have given them, saith the Lord thy God (Amos 9:15).

Now we might multiply passage upon passage almost indefinitely in this same vein and along this same line to show how clearly the Lord has revealed that in this millennial age when Christ shall have dominion on this earth, Israel will be restored and be redeemed forever from her dispersion. We must needs give one more passage to drive home and clinch the certainty of this event. God says that there is more possibility of the sun ceasing to shine or the stars of heaven failing to give their light, than that He should ever cast off the seed of Israel that they should not be restored in the land. God said it would be easier to measure the heavens and the foundations of the earth to be searched out, than that Israel should ever be brought to naught. Here is the record as we have it in Jeremiah thirty-one:

> Thus saith the Lord, which giveth the sun for a light

by day, and the ordinances of the moon and of the stars for a light by night, which divideth the sea when the waves thereof roar; The Lord of hosts is his name:

If those ordinances depart from before me, saith the Lord, then the seed of Israel also shall cease from being a nation before me for ever.

Thus saith the Lord; If heaven above can be measured, and the foundations of the earth searched out beneath, I will also cast off all the seed of Israel for all that they have done, saith the Lord (Jeremiah 31:35-37).

We trust we have not wearied you by the multiplication of Scripture quotations which we have been giving you, but we have been exceedingly eager that you might see how clear the Word of the Lord is in regard to His plan and program in the millennial age for the land of Palestine and for His ancient people, Israel. One cannot quite understand how anyone with an open Bible can fail to see the definite and clear outline which God has given concerning His program.

Way back in the book of Genesis, chapter twelve, God made an everlasting covenant of grace which cannot be broken, in which He promised to Abraham not only a seed, but a land, and the seed and the land were to be forever associated. Whenever Israel has been out of the land, the world has been in turmoil and in trouble. Only as Israel is at rest and peace in the land, acknowledging her God and serving her Messiah, can this world ever hope for peace. As man seeks for a solution to all of his problems, he fails to realize that the entire solution lies in acknowledging God's program with regard to His ancient people and His ancient Holy Land. As long as Jerusalem, the city of peace, is not at peace, there can be no peace in the world. Soon the Lord Jesus Christ, however, will come, and He will put to naught all the enemies of the Lord and of His program and set up that glorious Kingdom for which every child of God is looking more and more each day. "Even so, come, Lord Jesus."

Truly, as we look upon conditions in the world today,

if we did not have this hope of Christ's returning, and we had to rely upon the power of the church and the testimony of Christians today to bring about the cessation of all hostilities and bring in perfect righteousness, we should despair and give up hope. If I did not believe in the imminent, personal return of the Lord Jesus Christ to make right that which is wrong, and to bring in the peace for which man has so long been sighing and for which he has been so long looking, I should never preach another sermon. I would have to admit that the whole thing is a failure, and that the Gospel has not accomplished that which we had expected it to do, and that Christianity is nothing else but another religion, and a tremendous farce.

Glory be to God, we have this assurance that He who said He would come will come and will not tarry. His last promise which He left with His disciples was "I am coming again." The last promise in the Bible is, "He which testifieth these things saith, Surely I come quickly."

We praise God that, in the midst of all the darkening shadows of impending judgment and the ominous rumbling of the dark days ahead when men's hearts are failing them for fear of things which are coming to pass upon the earth, we dare to believe for ourselves that everything is going to be all right. We thank God that we can believe He is still on the throne, that His program is being carried out in this world, and that soon He will come and take away the veil and explain all which today remains so dark to us. We are not only happy we can believe that for ourselves, and rejoice in the infinite comfort which it brings to our own hearts, but we thank God for the blessed privilege and opportunity of being able to bring it to others, to broadcast this message to a lost world, the message of hope and cheer which the world needs so much today.

What a glorious message it is to bring to a world which today is floundering about in dismay and in confusion, not knowing whither to turn, and the darker the days become, the more glorious this blessed hope shines in our lives. I come to you with a message of encouragement and hope and assurance and cheer, that one of these days, just as sure as Jesus came to die on the Cross, He is coming again. He is coming again to put a stop to all of the wickedness and all of the inequality and the iniquity of this present age, to put an end to man's rule of failure and bungling, and to set up His glorious, millennial kingdom. Yes, indeed, one of these days:

> The Lord Himself shall descend from heaven with a shout, with the voice of the archangel, and with the trump of God: and the dead in Christ shall rise first:
>
> Then we which are alive and remain shall be caught up together with them in the clouds, to meet the Lord in the air: and so shall we ever be with the Lord.
>
> Wherefore comfort one another with these words (I Thessalonians 4:16-18).
>
> For thus saith the Lord; Sing with gladness for Jacob, and shout among the chief of the nations: publish ye, praise ye, and say, O Lord, save thy people, the remnant of Israel.
>
> Behold, I will bring them from the north country, and gather them from the coasts of the earth, and with them the blind and the lame, the woman with child and her that travaileth with child together: a great company shall return thither.
>
> They shall come with weeping, and with supplications will I lead them: I will cause them to walk by the rivers of waters in a straight way, wherein they shall not stumble: for I am a father to Israel, and Ephraim is my firstborn.
>
> Hear the word of the Lord, O ye nations, and declare it in the isles afar off, and say, He that scattered Israel will gather him, and keep him, as a shepherd doth his flock (Jeremiah 31:7-10).

Or listen to this word of comfort, spoken in the same connection, in Joel three:

> And it shall come to pass in that day, that the mountains

shall drop down new wine, and the hills shall flow with milk, and all the rivers of Judah shall flow with waters, and a fountain shall come forth of the house of the Lord, and shall water the valley of Shittim.

But Judah shall dwell for ever, and Jerusalem from generation to generation (Joel 3:18, 20).

We must realize that this is the Word of the Lord, and since there is so much of denial of the prophetic truth that Israel will be literally restored again to their land in the millennial age, we multiply these passages, trusting they will make an impression upon your heart. Here is another found in Amos nine:

Behold, the days come, saith the Lord, that the plowman shall overtake the reaper, and the treader of grapes him that soweth seed; and the mountains shall drop sweet wine, and all the hills shall melt.

And I will bring again the captivity of my people of Israel, and they shall build the waste cities, and inhabit them; and they shall plant vineyards, and drink the wine thereof; they shall also make gardens, and eat the fruit of them.

Why say ye not a word of bringing back the King?
  Why speak ye not of Jesus and His reign?
Why tell ye of His kingdom and of its glory sing,
  But nothing of His coming back again?

Dost thou not want to look upon His loving face?
  Dost thou not want to see Him glorified?
Wouldst thou not hear His welcome, and in that very place,
  Where years ago we saw Him crucified?

Oh, hark, creation's groans how can thou be assuaged,
  How can our bodies know redemptive joy?
How can the war be ended in which we are engaged,
  Until He come, the lawless to destroy?

Come quickly, blessed Lord, our hearts a welcome hold;
  We long to see creation's second birth.
Thy promise of Thy coming to some is growing cold.
  Oh, hasten thy returning back to earth.

"EVEN SO, COME, LORD JESUS"

Chapter Nineteen

THE WITHERED FIG TREE

THE BIBLE ABOUNDS WITH FIGURES and pictures of the program of God in relation to the nation of Israel, with whom God established His covenant through Abraham, Isaac and Jacob. In the Chapters so far we have been considering this program of God as revealed in the vision of the Valley of Dry Bones, as given to the prophet in the thirty-seventh chapter of Ezekiel. The vision of the Valley of Dry Bones is only one of many other Scriptures which teach this same truth concerning Israel's past, present and future. The Lord Jesus Christ Himself, during His ministry here upon earth, gave us one of the most graphic pictures of the future of the nation to whom He had come to offer the kingdom, but by whom He had been rejected. The cursing of the fig tree is not only a miracle, but it becomes in the light of all the rest of the Bible a parable which teaches the same identical truth as the vision of the Valley of Dry Bones. We trust that we shall be able to show in these messages the similarity and the unity of teaching in both of these instances given by the same Holy Spirit in the Old Testament as well as the New.

> Now in the morning as he returned into the city, he hungered.
> And when he saw a fig tree in the way, he came to it, and found nothing thereon, but leaves only, and said unto it, Let no fruit grow on thee henceforward forever. And presently the fig tree withered away.

And when the disciples saw it, they marvelled, saying, How soon is the fig tree withered away (Matthew 21:18-20).

This is Matthew's account of the miracle of the withered fig tree. The evangelist Mark also records the same incident and adds some details which are omitted by Matthew, such as the information that Jesus saw the fig tree afar off and also that it was not yet time for figs to appear. The miracle was performed a few days before Jesus was to go to the Cross to be crucified, and followed almost immediately the triumphal entry on Palm Sunday. In the interval between Jesus' entry into Jerusalem riding on an asses' colt, and this cursing of the fig tree, we have Jesus entering the temple and driving out the money changers, accusing them of making the house of God into a den of thieves. All of the detail about this setting is important if we are to understand the meaning of the withering of the fig tree. At the final offer of Jesus to be their king, He was rejected by the leaders of the nation of Israel, and so He turns His back upon them, drives them from Jehovah's temple and then leaves the city, never to return to spend another night there until the night of His trial.

JESUS LEAVES JERUSALEM

It is significant to notice that Jesus refuses, after this rejection, to abide in the city of Jerusalem. While He returns in the morning to teach and show Himself in the city, He leaves the city at night and abides rather in the city of Bethany. He has been rejected by the nation, they have refused their King, and the kingdom itself is now postponed and Jesus, the King, prepares to go to the Cross but refuses to abide in the city of the king and goes instead outside the camp to bear the sin of the world.

It was on His return from the city at eventide that He caused the fig tree to wither and die. It is important to remember these details. Jesus is now finally rejected for the last time, and soon the leaders will call down God's curse upon themselevs when they cry "His blood be on us and on our children." To illustrate the rejection of the nation, Jesus performs the miracle of the withered fig tree.

The fig tree is Israel, the nation which, when their Messiah came, did not recognize Him, but rejected Him. Now in the program of God they are to be set aside for a time, without fruit, out of the land, wandering among the nations, until the time of their restoration.

CURSED FOR THE AGE

The words of our Lord in cursing the fig tree are significant. He says: "No man eat fruit of thee hereafter for ever" (Mark 11:14).

Matthew quotes Jesus as saying the same thing. It is misunderstanding of this verse which has caused so much confusion in regard to the revelation concerning the restoration of Israel. Those who do not accept the literal fulfillment of prophecy, but spiritualize the promises to Israel, tell us that God is all through with Israel as a nation, and they will never again be restored to their land. They tell us that the church now is spiritual Israel and all the prophecies to the nation must be interpreted symbolically and spiritually as applying to so-called spiritual Israel, and they base their argument in part upon this verse, which says "Let no fruit grow on thee hereafter for ever." "Forever," they tell us, means that God is done with the nation *forever*. This misunderstanding is unfortunate and is due to a simple *mistranslation* of the word "forever." The word translated *forever* is *aion* in the Greek original, and means an *age*, a period of time, or a dispensation. So what Jesus really said was "Let no fruit grow on thee for an age, or a dispensation, for a period of time." As we shall see, the withering of the fig tree was only temporary and not permanent. This is suggested first of all by the account in Mark. Mark tells us a very interesting detail, which is well worth repeating: "And in the morning, as they passed by, they saw the fig tree dried up from the roots" (Mark 11:20).

The last three words of this verse tell the story. *From the roots.* Remember *from* the roots. In other words, the trunk and the branches and the leaves all withered away, but *not the roots*. The root remained alive while the rest withered away. Now the trunk and branches and leaves are the visible part of the tree, the roots are beneath the ground and are the invisible part of the tree. The upper part man sees, the roots God sees. Now the future of the fig tree as representing the nation of Israel is rooted in *God's* eternal Covenant with Abraham and with Isaac and with Jacob. This was a covenant of grace, an everlasting covenant which cannot be broken. God had said to Abraham concerning his seed:

> And I will establish my covenant between me and thee and thy seed after thee in their generations for an everlasting covenant, to be a God unto thee, and to thy seed after thee.
> And I will give unto thee, and to thy seed after thee, the land wherein thou art a stranger, all the land of Canaan, for an everlasting possession (Genesis 17:7-8).

Surely language could be no plainer than that. This covenant was confirmed to Isaac, then to Jacob, then to Moses and then to David, and repeated over and over again by the prophets even after Israel had gone into the dispersion. Paul tells us this covenant still holds when he says in Romans 11:25-27:

> For I would not, brethren, that ye should be ignorant of this mystery, lest ye should be wise in your own conceits; that blindness in part is happened to Israel, until (*until, until*) the fulness of the Gentiles be come in.
> And so all Israel shall be saved: as it is written, There shall come out of Sion the Deliverer, and shall turn away ungodliness from Jacob:
> For this is my covenant unto them, when I shall take away their sins.

Yes, the fig tree is withered, but only *until* the fulness

of the Gentiles be come in, for God remembers His covenant with them and the fig tree shall blossom and bear fruit again, and even today the buds are already appearing upon the tree. For the first time in 2500 years, Israel is recognized by the nations with her own president and her own flag and her own currency and her rightful name, Israel. All this is suggested by the detail given by Mark. The fig tree was dried up *from* the roots, but the root of God's covenant can never be broken. God will keep His word to Abraham, Isaac and Jacob. Sooner shall the sun cease to shine or the moon fail to give her light than that God should fail in the promise of the final restoration of Israel as a nation in the land of Canaan and the planting of the fig tree in the land of Jehovah. That at least is the way Jeremiah puts it:

> Thus saith the Lord, which giveth the sun for a light by day, and the ordinances of the moon and of the stars for a light by night . . .
> If those ordinances depart from before me, saith the LORD, then the seed of Israel also shall cease from being a nation before me for ever.
> Thus saith the Lord; If heaven above can be measured, and the foundations of the earth searched out beneath, I will also cast off all the seed of Israel for all that they have done, saith the Lord (Jeremiah 31:35-37).

It is a serious thing to deny that the fig tree Israel will ever again be restored as a nation in the land of Palestine, for it is in direct violation of the clear simple teaching of the Word of God. Yes, even though withered now, it will yet blossom and bud and bring forth fruit, and right today we see the first buds of promise appearing.

SUPERNATURALLY PRESERVED

In Scripture, the nation of Israel is represented not only by the fig tree but two other trees, the olive and the vine. Isaiah tells us:

> For the vineyard of the Lord of hosts is the house of Israel, and the men of Judah his pleasant plant: and he

looked for judgment, but behold oppression; for righteousness, but behold a cry (Isaiah 5:7).

Israel is the vine of the Lord, but according to Jesus it brought forth wild grapes and, therefore, the vineyard of the Lord has been delivered, to be scattered, and like the fig tree, withered from the roots. It will one day sprout again and bring forth its abundant fruit. Again, Paul compares the nation of Israel to an olive tree whose branches have been broken off because of their unbelief, but who shall be grafted in again when they repent and turn to the Lord. These three trees, therefore, teach the lesson of the fig tree. And all of them are summed up in the teaching of the burning bush which Moses met on the backside of the desert. Ever burning but never, never consumed, because God's covenant cannot fail and though the tree may wither, the roots remain firm in the faithfulness of their covenant-keeping God.

THIS GENERATION SHALL NOT PASS

Jesus said concerning this nation of the fig tree, that it would never perish until all the Word of God concerning her has been fulfilled. In Matthew Jesus says:

> Now learn a parable of the fig tree; When his branch is yet tender, and puteth forth leaves, ye know that summer is nigh:
> So likewise ye, when ye shall see all these things, know that it is near, even at the doors.
> Verily I say unto you, This generation shall not pass, till all these things be fulfilled.
> Heaven and earth shall pass away, but my words shall not pass away (Matthew 24:32-35).

Notice Jesus' words, *"This generation shall not pass, till all these things be fulfilled."* Literally, Jesus says, *this nation,* represented by the fig tree, shall never cease to be until all these things be fulfilled. The word translated *Generation* is the word *Genea* in the original

Greek, and denotes a people or nation. We may, therefore, read Jesus' words as follows, "This people or nation shall never pass (or perish) till all these things be fulfilled." History stands as irrevocable testimony to the truth of this word. This people indeed have been the indestructible nation of the Lord, who, like the burning bush, have been in the fires of persecution for all these centuries but never, never destroyed. Though reduced at one time to less than one million in the world, God has kept His Word and supernaturally preserved them according to His sure promise. The existence of every single member of the nation of Israel is incontrovertible proof of the truth of the Bible and the eternal character of God's Word.

Soon the Fig Tree Will Revive

We believe with all our hearts that we are living in the very days when the fig tree is being revived and the dry bones of the house of Israel are beginning to move and come together. To the Bible student of prophecy, the most significant sign of the Coming of the Lord is the recent activity in the nation of Israel. The most important event from the standpoint of prophecy is not the discovery of the atomic bomb, nor the revival of the Roman Empire as we see it in the United Nations, nor even the rise of the King of the North as represented by Russia. Overshadowing everything else is this fulfillment of the Word of God that in our own time and generation we have seen a nation, scattered and without a land or national existence for nearly 2500 years, suddenly asserting itself and in the face of the greatest and gravest odds taking her place among the peoples of the earth as the *Nation of Israel*. Overlooked by many, I repeat, this is the most significant event in our generation, verifying the Word of God, heralding the coming of the Christ who said,

Now learn a parable of the fig tree; when his branch is yet tender, and putteth forth leaves, ye know that summer is nigh:

So likewise ye, when ye shall see all these things, know that it (the coming of the Lord) is near, even at the doors.

Verily I say unto you, This generation (nation) shall not pass, until all these things be fulfilled (Matthew 24:32-34).

Chapter Twenty

Nothing But Leaves

And on the morrow, when they were come from Bethany, he was hungry:

And seeing a fig tree afar off having leaves, he came, if haply he might find anything thereon: and when he came to it, he found nothing but leaves; for the time of figs was not yet.

And Jesus answered and said unto it, No man eat fruit of thee hereafter for ever. And his disciples heard it (Mark 11:12-14).

And when even was come, he went out of the city.

And in the morning, as they passed by, they saw the fig tree dried up from the roots.

And Peter calling to remembrance saith unto him, Master, behold, the fig tree which thou cursedst is withered away.

And Jesus answering saith unto them, Have faith in God. (Mark 11:19-22).

THE ONLY THING THE LORD JESUS ever cursed while he was here on the earth was this fig tree, mentioned not only here, but also in the Gospel through Matthew. The Holy Spirit considered the teaching of the withered fig tree of such importance that He inspired not one, but two of the evangelists to preserve the details of the record for us. It behooves us, therefore, to study carefully the teaching of an incident which the Holy Spirit Himself deemed so important that He repeats it in two of the Gospel records. The reason given why the Lord cursed this fig tree was not because it had leaves, but because it had nothing *but* leaves. It was *not* cursed for having leaves, but for *not* having fruit when there were already leaves on the tree.

Fig leaves in the Bible always represent a *profession* without fruit. It is a picture of false religion and profession without the fruit of salvation. This we gather from the first time fig leaves are mentioned in the Bible. The first time fig leaves are mentioned in the Scriptures is in Genesis three. After the fall of our first parents, instead of fleeing to God for His covering for their sin, they resorted to the making of fig leaf aprons to cover their nakedness. It was man's first attempt to make himself presentable to God by his own labor and work and effort. It is a picture of *religion,* the effort of man to dress himself up in moral clothes by religion, morality, reformation, ritual, ceremony and good works, the while refusing the gift of God through faith by grace.

Fig leaves then represent, according to this rule, the rejection of God's remedy for sin and the setting up of a human righteousness of *law, works* and *religion,* with great profession but no spiritual fruit. This is the thing which Jesus cursed on the way from Jerusalem to Bethany. Jesus never cursed a sinner, a harlot a thief or a robber. You may search your Bible from Matthew one to the end of the book and you will find that our Saviour had nothing but tenderness, pity, compassion and forgiveness for the poor, defiled, fallen sinner, but when it came to religious self-righteousness, no condemnation was too strong.

In Matthew twenty-three, when speaking to the religious, self-righteous Pharisees and Scribes, all dressed up in their fig leaf aprons of legality and religion, He castigates them in a way which surprises us as we listen to the gentle Jesus who could be so patient and kind with lost men and women. He calls these tailors of fig leaf suits snakes, "a generation of vipers." He compares them to white plastered graves, all white and clean on the outside, but inside full of corruption and dead men's bones. Fig leaves without fruit. He accuses them of cleaning the outside of the plate and platter but within being filled with filth. He says they strain at a little gnat, but are able to swallow a great big camel. He condemns their religious zeal in no uncertain terms when He says, "Ye compass sea and land to make one proselyte, and when he is made, ye make him twofold more the child of hell than yourselves."

Yes, the only thing Jesus ever cursed was the fig tree and those whom the fig tree represents. Religious hypocrisy seems to be the sin Christ hates above all things. Religious self-righteousness and bigotry is the stench in the nostrils of the Almighty. Someone has said, Jesus came to save men from two things, *sin and religion,* and religion is by far the greater sin of the two. It is a hundred times easier to lead a fallen sinner to Christ than these religious professors. The man in the gutter needs not be told very often that he needs salvation. He knows it. But how to reach these pious, religious pretenders who are so good in their legalism that they feel no need for Christ, is a problem which is difficult to solve. They will draw their pretty fig leaves about them and seem utterly impervious to the penetration of the Gospel of human sinfulness and the utter corruptness of the human unregenerate heart. Jesus said to one of the best, most religious, moral, lawabiding men of His time, Nicodemus, "Except a man be born again, he cannot see the kingdom of God."

The Fig Tree Is Israel

The teaching of the fig tree has not only a practical lesson for us, but when Jesus caused the fig tree to wither He was also teaching a prophetic lesson with regard to the future of the nation of Israel to whom He came as their Messiah and Saviour. To understand this dispensational and prophetic teaching, we must call attention first of all to the setting of this miracle.

Jesus was facing the Cross. It is a few days before Calvary and His rejection and crucifixion at the hands of the elders and Scribes and Pharisees. In the first part of the chapter, we have the record of Christ's last official offer to Israel to be their king. Thirty-three years before, He had come into the world and the angel had announced Him as the One who would sit on the throne of His father David and rule over the house of Jacob forever. Then, at thirty, He began His public ministry and His message was the kingdom, "Repent ye for the kingdom of heaven is at hand." This message was only for the nation of Israel and for no other. Notice carefully in Matthew ten that when Jesus sent out His disciples with this message He gave strict orders that this offer and message was for Israel only and *not for the Gentiles.* Here are Jesus' words:

> These twelve Jesus sent forth, and commanded them, saying, Go not into the way of the Gentiles, and into any city of the Samaritans enter ye not:
> But go rather to the lost sheep of the house of Israel.
> And as ye go, preach, saying, The kingdom of heaven is at hand.
> Heal the sick, cleanse the lepers, raise the dead, cast out devils: freely ye have received, freely give (Matthew 10: 5-8).

It was the offer of the kingdom, it was only for Israel and verified and confirmed by kingdom miracles and signs, and had nothing to do with the nations, the Gentiles or the church. For three and a half years the message went forth only to meet with rejection from the very ones for whom it was meant. In fulfillment of prophecy, "He came unto his own, and his own received him not."

Now this rejected Messiah has come to the end of His ministry and in a few days will be crucified, His message spurned and He Himself rejected by the Jews. But, that there might be no excuse for them, Jesus first gives them one more offer of the kingdom in His official offer recorded in Matthew 21, Mark 11, and again in Luke 10. This is usually referred to as the *triumphal entry on palm sunday,* but it was nothing of the sort. It was not His triumphal entry for it led to His rejection and the Cross. The triumphal entry of Jesus into Jerusalem will take place when He comes again according to Zechariah 14 and Revelation 19, when he returns to His waiting nation of Israel and will set up the kingdom when those who there rejected Him will cry out from their hearts with true understanding, "Hosanna to the Son of David: Blessed is he that cometh in the name of the Lord; Hosanna in the highest" (Matthew 21:9).

It is right after this rejection of Jesus Christ as He offered Himself to Israel as their king for the final time that the incident of the withered fig tree occurs and therefore gives us the key to its meaning. The fig tree is the nation which rejected Him, the nation of Israel through its leaders the Pharisees, Scribes and rulers of the people. The Messiah is rejected and as a result the nation is set aside to be withered and scattered.

THE SIN OF ISRAEL

The reason the nation of Israel was rejected by the Lord was for the same reason the fig tree was cursed. It was because it had leaves without fruit. Leaves speak of man's efforts to justify himself, man's religion of good works while rejecting the remedy, the only remedy for sin, the blood of God's Substitute. The leaders of Israel in Jesus' day were indeed covered with fig leaves. They said, "We be Abraham's seed, and were never in bondage to any man." They prided themselves in their religious perfection, as they tithed of mint and anise and cummin, as they strained out a tiny gnat for fear they should be religiously defiled. They boasted of their law keeping and their punctual observance of the sabbath day, but all to no avail for they rejected the Son of God their Saviour and their Messiah. Fig leaves without fruit.

Paul in writing of this same thing in Romans says of the people who were his kinsmen according to the flesh,

> For they being ignorant of God's righteousness, and going about to establish their own righteousness, have not submitted themselves to the righteousness of God (Romans 10:3).

In brief, *fig leaves,* pleading their own righteousness instead of God's righteousness. So religious were these leaders that when Jesus was tried in Pilate's court, they would not enter this Gentile court lest they defile themselves religiously, while all the while they were crying for the blood of the Son of God. They were zealous for the tradition of the fathers, but rejecting their fathers' God.

THE TIME OF FIGS WAS NOT YET

We are further told that when Jesus saw this tree, it was not yet time for figs. It was too early in the season. It was not time for fruit as yet. Still Jesus looked for fruit even though our Scripture says plainly, "for the time of figs was not yet." Does it not seem unjust and unfair for Jesus to look for figs at a time when there were no figs on the trees, in late winter or early spring? Yes, it would have been, except for one thing, *it had leaves, it professed to have fruit.* If it was so early in the season, what business did this tree have showing *leaves*? This was the only deciduous tree in the whole country that was covered with leaves. All the rest of the trees were still dormant, without leaves. Not only is this suggested by the fact that it was not yet time for figs, but also in the statement in verse thirteen. Notice it carefully: "And seeing a fig tree afar off having leaves."

Do not miss that. He saw the tree *afar off having leaves. Afar off,* that is, a long way off. He could see it afar off because it had leaves while the rest of the trees were still bare. In that landscape with bare trees, that fig tree covered with leaves stuck out like a sore thumb, and could be seen a mile away. Naturally, if this precocious tree had leaves when it was not time, the Lord could expect figs as well, and when He found none, He cursed it and it withered away.

He did not curse the other trees. They had no more fruit on them than this fig tree, but they made no pretence of having fruit for they did not display any leaves. Leaves are profession, fruit represents possession and salvation. This is the thing God hates, a profession without a salvation. Religion without Christ, faith without works, a testimony without life. Because the nation of Israel professed much religion and made their boast of the Law and their own righteousness but rejected the Saviour, our Lord cursed the tree, until that day, as we shall see in our subsequent chapters, when they shall "look on Him whom they have pierced" and shall acknowledge and receive the Messiah and the curse shall be removed and the withered, scattered and peeled nation of the fig tree shall be gathered again and planted in the land of Canaan and sprout and blossom and bring forth fruit, until the face of the earth shall be filled with its fruit and Israel shall be the joy and praise of all the earth.

The lesson is also ours, that religion without Christ is an abomination. Without personal, saving faith in Jesus Christ, the Son of God, everything is but empty fig leaves. Religion, ordinances, ritual, church membership, sacraments, good works, lawkeeping and everything else without being born again, are but fig leaves, only to be cursed by Him who cursed the fig tree, and the One who said to one of the finest, moral and religious characters of His day, Nicodemus, "Marvel not that I said unto thee, Ye must be born again."

Chapter Twenty-one

RELIGION OR SALVATION

> And on the morrow, when they were come from Bethany,
> he was hungry:
> And seeing a fig tree afar off having leaves, he came, if
> haply he might find any thing thereon: and when he came
> to it, he found nothing but leaves; for the time of figs was
> not yet.
> And Jesus answered and said unto it, No man eat fruit
> of thee hereafter for ever. And his disciples heard it.
> (Mark 11:12-14).

NOTHING BUT LEAVES. Such is the description of the fig
tree on the way from Bethany to Jerusalem, and because
it had nothing but leaves the fig tree was cursed and
withered away. Nothing but leaves. There is nothing
wrong with a fig tree having leaves; a healthy fig tree
should have leaves, but the trouble with this fig tree
was that it had nothing *but leaves.* They were undoubtedly
very beautiful leaves, luxuriant and prominent, for Mark
is careful to tell us that Jesus saw the fig tree *afar off.*
It was a prominent tree and its leaves stood out clearly,
so that they were evident to all who passed by. Yet Jesus
cursed the tree, *not* because it had leaves but because it
had *nothing but leaves.*

REFERS TO ISRAEL

The primary interpretation of this miracle of Jesus in
cursing the tree is to the nation of Israel, who through

its leaders had rejected Him, the Son of God, and in a few days would demand His death by crucifixion. Israel is the withered fig tree which, while withered from the *roots up,* is nevertheless never destroyed completely but supernaturally preserved until the day of her national revival and conversion, then to become the fruitful plant of Jehovah in the land of Canaan, promised to them by an everlasting covenant. This interpretation by no means exhausts the teaching of the fig tree, and so, before we take up in our next chapter the budding and revival of the fig tree, we wish to devote this one chapter to a very practical application. Fig leaves in the Bible represent man's own effort to make himself fit for the presence of God. It represents *human* righteousness as opposed to divine righteousness. Fig leaves represent *religion* without life, a profession without possession, a claim without reality, a form of godliness, but denying the power thereof.

ADAM AND EVE

The first time fig leaves are mentioned in the Bible occurs in Genesis three. Our first parents, Adam and Eve, had broken with God, had fallen in sin and were under the sure judgment and condemnation of God, who had said, "The day that thou eatest thereof thou shalt surely die." Adam, instead of recognizing the fact that no outward cleansing, no outside decorations could make him fit for God's presence, but only a divine work of grace, instead of crying and fleeing to God for salvation, hid himself in the garden and began to fashion a garment of his own manufacture, a religion of works, a salvation by human effort and toil, only to find that he could not *cover* his sin in the sight of God by anything less than God's own garment of righteousness, provided only by the death of an innocent substitute and by the shedding of blood.

GOD FINDS ADAM

It is God who seeks Adam, instead of Adam seeking after God. He finds him in the garden, sewing fig leaves together and seeking to cover himself with religion instead of with the garment of salvation. This is the meaning of the fig leaves. They represent every effort of man to justify himself by his own works: religion, church membership, ordinances, culture, refinement and morality, *without personal saving* faith in Jesus Christ and His atoning substitutionary sacrifice for sinners.

Right after Adam had made an attempt to cover himself with the fig leaves of his own works, God showed him the only way of salvation. In Genesis 3:21, we have the first mention in the Bible of an acceptable covering for man's sin. Here is the familiar verse, "Unto Adam also and to his wife did the Lord God make coats of skins, and clothed them."

Here is God's covering for sin in contrast to man's efforts by fig leaves. Notice, there are just three things suggested in this verse and we want to emphasize them, although we have mentioned them many times before. Note these well:

1. Salvation must be the work of God—not man. It is God who makes the coats of skins. Adam had no part in it at all.

2. It must be by the death of a substitute. The penalty of sin was death and since God cannot lie, the death penalty must be paid. Since God is a Saviour and wants men to be saved, He provides a substitute for Adam. God takes an animal, probably a lamb, and takes its life. All this is implied by the fact that God took the *skins* of an animal. To procure the skin involved the death of the animal. Now we come to the third condition.

3. Salvation must be by the shedding of blood. Since life is in the blood (Leviticus 17:17), death means that the blood died. Sin affected the blood of man, the one

bond which unites all men. In order to pay the penalty of death, and restore life, blood must be provided—not the blood of the guilty one, but the blood of an innocent victim.

GOD'S REQUIREMENT FOR REDEMPTION

Here, then, in the very dawn of history almost immediately after Adam had sinned, God lays down the inviolable rule of salvation. It must be by the death of a substitute, and it must be by the shedding of the blood of an innocent victim. God knows no other way of salvation. Anything which man invents, his effort to leave out one of these three, is an abomination before the Lord and leads to eternal damnation.

THE ORDER NEVER CHANGES

This threefold requirement of acceptable sacrifice, in contrast to man's efforts at providing his own covering of fig leaves, has never changed. Salvation is still of the Lord and "without shedding of blood is no remission" (Hebrews 9:22). We have a striking illustration of this in the very next chapter. Adam and Eve had two sons, Cain and Abel. Cain believed in fig leaves, Abel believed in God's substitute and redemption through blood. Cain was by far the most religious of the two but ended in hell. Abel simply believed God's word as illustrated in the coats of skins and is today in heaven. And these two men are representative of *religion* and *salvation.* Cain believed in *religion,* works and human merit, Abel believed in God's provided Lamb. Cain brought the labor of his own hands, the fruit of the field, and was rejected; Abel brought God's lamb and was accepted.

We could trace this all the way through the Bible. Noah brought a sacrifice to the Lord of the clean animals. It was God's substitute and was by shedding of blood. Then when Israel left Egypt, God impressed upon them this great truth by giving them the most elaborate tabernacle ritual and later their temple worship. This ritual centered around the *altar,* as the place of sacrifice. It was a ritual of substitution, sacrifice, and of blood, as the countless thousands of animals were slain and the blood flowed in an unbroken stream from the tabernacle gates. Yet when God's true Lamb came, they did not recognize Him, for "He came unto his own, and his own received him not."

They resorted once again to fig leaves, rejected God's sacrificial passover Lamb, and as a result Israel, the fig tree, is rejected and withers away until that glad day when they shall accept God's Lamb and be saved.

PRACTICAL APPLICATION

Human nature has not changed since that day, and man is still being deceived by the curse of a bloodless religion. The preaching of a social gospel without the blood of Christ is but a repetition of the fig leaves of Adam and Eve. The modern teaching that we do not have to believe the infallible inspiration of the Bible or the supernatural conception of Jesus, or His Virgin Birth, is only again man hiding from the truth in the garden of his fall and seeking to sew fig leaf aprons. The teaching that we all have a spark of the divine in us and it only needs culture and development is in direct violation of the clear teaching of the Word of God which says, that we are *"dead in sins"* and that "There is none righteous, no, not one" (Romans 3:10). The error of believing that man must keep the law to be saved or even to *remain* saved is only disappointing wishful thinking which ignores the depravity of the Adamic nature in each and every one of us, and is the story of fig leaves all over again.

The most important question which can be asked, is, Have you been born again? Do not confuse religion with the new birth. It was to a very religious man that Jesus said, "Marvel not that I said unto thee, Ye must be born again" (John 3:7).

But He Was Not Saved

He was a Pharisee, a respected man, a ruler among the people, a teacher in Israel, a religious man, but he did not know about the new birth and he was not saved. He had religion and it did not satisfy. He was earnest and sincere and had done all in his power to find peace and satisfaction in religion, but it left him without assurance and peace. He just had to keep on working and hoping, but it left an empty void, and a dreadful fear of the future. Here was a man who was not satisfied with mere religion, he wanted Christ. Herein Nicodemus was different than Cain, and the lost thief on the cross. He recognized that externals are not enough and that all his goodness, while it might impress those about him, would not fit him to stand in the presence of God in the end. As we have stated before, religion without Christ is dead, because only Christianity has a living head. Webster's dictionary defines religion as follows, "a system of rules of conduct and laws of action based upon the recognition of, and belief in, and a reverence for, a superhuman power of supreme authority." Notice carefully the definition as given. It is a system of rules for conduct and action, produced by a belief in a superhuman power of supreme authority. Everyone, then, who believes in a higher power or a god, whether personal or impersonal, is a religious person. That superhuman power may be the sun, the moon, a sacred cow, even a serpent. It may be a river, or a man, or an image of wood or stone or metal. According to the meaning of the word religion, any belief in a power higher than human makes a man religious.

Religion or Salvation?

You see, then, there are only two ways, the way of man and the way of God. Man's way is the religious way; God's way is the simple way of grace. Man's way is by fig leaves of his own making; God's way is the way of sacrifice and the blood of the Lamb. Man's way is by works, God's way is by faith. Man's way is by religion; God's way is by believing. "There is a way that seemeth right unto a man, but the end thereof are the ways of death." Jesus said: "I am the way, the truth, and the life: no man cometh unto the Father, but by me" (John 14:6).

"Are *you* religious or are you saved?" If you merely have religion and have never come by the way of the blood of Christ, then you are still in your sins. God calls to you today to answer His question. When Adam hid in the garden God came and called to him and said, "Adam . . . where art thou? Why do you hide from me?" Poor Adam came out in his flimsy fig-leaf apron, still as guilty and still as lost as he was before. What is *your* hope of heaven? Ask yourself, or at least let me ask you. Are you sure of heaven? *Are you saved? Oh,* I hear one say, "I live a good life and do the best I can."

Fig leaves, just plain *fig leaves,* for God says, "There is none righteous, no, not one." Another says, "Well, I cannot understand the Bible." *Fig leaves.* God asks you to *believe,* and not to understand first of all. We shall never fully understand how God could give His pure and lovely Son to die for wicked sinners like us. Oh, you say, "I don't feel like I am saved." No, but salvation is not *feeling,* it is *believing.* Your feelings change every day, but God's promises are ever the same, and He says, "Whosoever believeth that Jesus is the Christ is born of God." You take my word for it, and trust Christ, and the feeling will come. You do not refuse food because you do not feel full. Eat your food and the feeling will come. All you need to feel is that you are lost, that you need a Saviour, and then come to Him and trust Him and the feeling will come. Cast aside your fig-leaf aprons and come under the shelter of His precious blood.

Chapter Twenty-two

THE BUDDING FIG TREE

Now learn a parable of the fig tree; When her branch is yet tender, and putteth forth leaves, ye know that summer is near:

So ye in like manner, when ye shall see these things come to pass, know that it is nigh, even at the doors.

Verily I say unto you, that this generation shall not pass, till all these things be done.

Heaven and earth shall pass away: but my words shall not pass away.

But of that day and that hour knoweth no man, no, not the angels which are in heaven, neither the Son, but the Father.

Take ye heed, watch and pray: for ye know not when the time is (Mark 13:28-33).

No SINGLE EVENT IN OUR PRESENT GENERATION has greater prophetic significance than the restoration of the nation of Israel in the land of Palestine. All of this was according to the prophecy which God had given in the covenant to Abraham, Isaac and Jacob. The prophecy was repeated hundreds of times throughout all the Old Testament by seers who foresaw that after the crucifixion of Christ and this present dispensation of the church of the Lord Jesus, Israel should again be re-gathered and restored in the land, never to be plucked up again.

THE BUDDING OF THE FIG TREE

It is a remarkable thing that we should be living in that very age when these things are beginning to come to pass before our eyes. In our past chapters we have been pointing out the fact that Jesus foretold all this under the figure and the parable of the miraculously withered but again-to-be-restored fig tree. We have seen how the fig tree was dried up from the roots, but the root itself, which is the covenant God made by grace with Abraham, Isaac and Jacob, has never been altered or changed. Even though the fig tree, Israel, has been withered for these nineteen hundred years since these words were spoken, nevertheless, the covenant of God is sure, and "the gifts and calling of God are without repentance."

We might occupy a great deal of time in showing how God has definitely promised that the nation, the natural seed of Abraham, through the Twelve Tribes of Israel, should finally be restored in the land of Palestine to become the center of the world governments with the Messiah reigning personally upon the Throne of David and bringing in peace and everlasting righteousness. In our Scripture taken from the thirteenth chapter of Mark, Jesus tells us that the fig tree is going to bud again. In this chapter our Lord is occupied with some of the events which shall immediately precede His second coming. Mark thirteen is in answer to the question of the disciples, concerning the time of His return and the end of the age, and in answer to this question Jesus gives a number of signs by which we may know that the end is very near.

Among these signs we have the increase of deception as we have it in verses five and six; then we have the prophecy of wars and rumors of wars, and the increase of famines and pestilences and earthquakes in divers places. Then we have also the prophecy that during these last days the Gospel shall be published among all nations, and we are living in the identical times when for the first time in history we are able by means of radio to send the Gospel message to the four corners of the earth, from pole to pole and to every nook and corner of this old world.

This has never been true before in all of history, and so we believe that we are living in the very days of the fulfillment of this prophecy.

THE FIRST SIGNS OF LIFE

It is in this connection that our Lord says: "Now learn a parable of the fig tree; When her branch is yet tender, and putteth forth leaves, ye know that summer is near" (Mark 13:28).

The one word in this verse which needs special emphasis is the definite article, "*the*," t h e. Our Lord did not say, now learn a parable of "a" fig tree, of "the fig trees," but He says definitely, "Now learn a parable of *the* fig tree." It is one particular, definite fig tree to which He is referring and no other. Of course, the disciples did not mistake the meaning of these words, and immediately their minds went back to the fig tree which had been withered only a day or so before at the word of the Lord Jesus Christ. Believing as we do that the fig tree is the nation of Israel, the Lord here gives as the indication of the last days the budding, the activity among the nation of Israel. And then adds: "So ye in like manner, when ye shall see these things come to pass, know that it is nigh, even at the doors" (Mark 13:29).

As we have already pointed out, the word "generation" here refers to the national existence of Israel. Jesus says that in spite of all the hatred of Satan and all the atrocities of world emperors of days gone by, and the rulers of darkness against this nation, beginning with Pharaoh in Egypt and coming all the way down the line through Nebuchadnezzar, Alexander, the Roman Empire, Hitler, Mussolini and many, many others, this nation will never cease until the promises of God have been completely fulfilled in their actual restoration in the land of Israel.

AN UP-TO-DATE PROPHECY

Today there is in the land of Palestine a nation which had been scattered for 2,500 years without a king of its own, without a national government of its own, without its own currency, without its own independent state, and yet today, we have seen it recognized among the nations. Truly, this is the budding of the fig tree. We recognize the fact that the present establishment of Israel in the land is not the fulfillment of the prophecy of the Word of God. This is a political move which, however, is an indication, the shadow and the preparation for, the final restoration when Israel shall be restored not only politically, but spiritually, and become the people and the choice of God. Not only a token and a remnant shall return to the land, but according to the sure Word of prophecy, every single son of Israel will return to the land, never to be plucked up again. There a remnant of them will become the messengers of God and the blessing of all the nations, and the Word of God spoken to Abraham will be finally and completely and ultimately fulfilled as He said: "In thy seed shall all the nations of the earth be blessed" (Genesis 22:18).

FULFILLMENT OF ISAIAH TWENTY-SIX

In this connection I would have you consider very carefully the prophecy spoken by the Lord through His Spirit in the twenty-sixth and twenty-seventh chapters of Isaiah. In the passage beginning at Isaiah 26:16 and ending with the close of the twenty-seventh chapter, we have a step-by-step account of the events which will follow upon the budding of the fig tree and the beginning of the restoration of Israel. I would that you might study this passage very, very carefully, for it is one of the outstanding, orderly passages of the Old Testament, in which we have the order of events as given by God Himself, ending up in the millennial rest and the peace of God as the Prince of Peace reigns in Jerusalem.

In the 16th, 17th and 18th verses of Isaiah twenty-six, we have the confession of Israel in the last days:

> Lord, in trouble have they visited thee, they poured out a prayer when thy chastening was upon them.
>
> Like as a woman with child, that draweth near the time of her delivery, is in pain, and crieth out in her pangs; so have we been in thy sight, O Lord (Isaiah 26:16-17).

Notice here that this is Israel speaking, with reference especially to the Tribulation period during which they will return to the Lord and will be accepted by Him as the people of His choice, and then we have their confession:

> We have been with child, (this is Israel speaking and confessing) we have been in pain, we have as it were brought forth wind; we have not wrought any deliverance in the earth; neither have the inhabitants of the world fallen (Isaiah 26:18).

Here we have the confession of Israel that their history has been merely a fulfillment of the fig tree which had leaves but no works. Here they confess that all of their efforts, that their own self-righteous attempts to justify themselves in the sight of God, have fallen short and have brought forth nothing but wind. They have not wrought any deliverance in the earth, neither have the inhabitants of the world fallen. This is the confession of Israel, according to the prophet Isaiah, when they shall acknowledge their sin, and shall repent before the Lord.

Notice very carefully what follows immediately upon this confession of Israel. In these verses we have seen the activity, the stirring as it were of the dry bones of the house of Israel. It is happening today in the fact that Israel has been crying and seeking a home land after the terrible atrocities of the past decade, and new hope is springing up within their hearts as they see their home land re-established. This is nothing short of the budding of the fig tree, and we are amazed as we see the 19th verse of the 26th chapter of Isaiah in which we have the next event after Israel begins to show its budding activity. Notice very carefully what we have in verse nineteen:

> Thy dead men shall live, together with my dead body shall they arise. Awake and sing, ye that dwell in the dust: for thy dew is as the dew of herbs, and the earth shall cast out the dead (Isaiah 26:19).

If we leave out the italicized words in this verse, "thy dead men shall live . . . my dead body shall they arise," then we have here a definite statement of the fact that immediately after the budding of the fig tree, the first resurrection will occur. "Thy dead men shall live . . . my dead body shall they arise." In the light of the context there can be no question but that this refers to the first resurrection at the return of Jesus Christ in the Rapture. Here we have God saying that His body which is the Church of Christ, shall arise very soon following the activity as represented here by Israel's confession. This is in harmony with the rest of Scriptures in which we read that the dead in Christ shall rise first. I Thessalonians 4:16 and again in I Corinthians 15:51, 52:

> Behold, I shew you a mystery; We shall not all sleep, but we shall all be changed,
> In a moment, in the twinkling of an eye, at the last trump: for the trumpet shall sound, and the dead shall be raised incorruptible, and we shall be changed.

THE RAPTURE OF THE CHURCH

Immediately following the first Resurrection at the coming of Christ will come the Rapture of the Church of Jesus Christ. We have this in Isaiah 26:20:

> Come, my people, enter thou into thy chambers, and shut thy doors about thee: hide thyself as it were for a little moment, until the indignation be overpast.

Here we have the third step. First we have the budding of the fig tree; then we have the first resurrection. Now we have the Rapture of the Church. Here we have the same words by the same one who spoke in Revelation four, when He said to John, "Come up hither." In this case it is the

Spirit again calling to His believers on the earth at the time of the second coming in the worlds: "Come, my people, enter thou into thy chambers." Jesus said in John 14: "In my Father's house are many mansions: if it were not so, I would have told you. I go to prepare a place for you."

Isaiah mentions the chambers which are synonymous with the many mansions which Christ is preparing today. This, then, is the Rapture of the Church of Jesus Christ. Then follows the fourth thing, the Tribulation, immediately after the Church has been taken out. Notice the order. First, the budding of the fig tree. Second, the Resurrection at Christ's coming. Then the Rapture of the Church, and then follows the Tribulation period. We read in Isaiah 26:20:

> "Hide thyself as it were for a little moment, until the indignation be overpast."

The word indignation here is another word for "the Tribulation"; also called the "Time of Jacob's Trouble," "the Day of the Lord," and "a day of clouds and of thick darkness." Immediately following the Rapture of the Church, we have the time of Tribulation which we believe will last for exactly seven years, between the Rapture and the Second Coming of Christ. Then comes event number five, the Second Coming of Christ in the Revelation at the close of the Tribulation period. We read in Isaiah 26:21:

> For, behold, the Lord cometh out of his place to punish the inhabitants of the earth for their iniquity: the earth also shall disclose her blood, and shall no more cover her slain.

We have two things in this verse, the Second Coming of the Lord and the Battle of Armageddon at the close of the Tribulation which will be terminated by the sudden appearance of our Saviour in the clouds of heaven. It is the battle of Armageddon which is at the close of the Tribulation period:

> The Lord cometh out of his place to punish the in-
> habitants of the earth for their iniquity: the earth also
> shall disclose her blood, and shall no more cover her
> slain (Isaiah 26:21).

So far, then, we have six events given in their exact
order. First, the budding of the fig tree. Second, the first
Resurrection at Jesus' coming. Third, the Rapture of the
Church after the first Resurrection. Fourth, the Great
Tribulation followed by the Second Coming of the Lord
Jesus Christ, and the culmination of the battle of Arma-
geddon. Now we come to event number seven, given
to us in Isaiah:

> In that day the Lord with his sore and great and strong
> sword shall punish leviathan the piercing serpent, even
> leviathan that crooked serpent; and he shall slay the dragon
> that is in the sea (Isaiah 27:1).

Here we have the binding of Satan at the setting up of
the kingdom at the Second Coming of the Lord Jesus
Christ. Leviathan, the piercing serpent, the crooked serpent, and the dragon, here are synonymous, of course, with
Satan and the devil. In the book of Revelation we read that
at the end of the Tribulation period and at the Second
Coming of the Lord Jesus Christ, John says:

> And I saw an angel come down from heaven, having
> the key of the bottomless pit and a great chain in his hand.
> And he laid hold on the dragon, that old serpent, which
> is the Devil, and Satan, and bound him a thousand years,
> And cast him into the bottomless pit, and shut him up,
> and set a seal upon him, that he should deceive the nations
> no more, till the thousand years should be fulfilled: and
> after that he must be loosed for a little season (Rev.
> 20:1-3).

Here then we have the event of which Isaiah speaks in
this chapter, the binding of Satan for one thousand years
during which:

> Jesus shall reign where'er the sun
>   Does his successive journeys run;
> His kingdom spread from shore to shore,
>   Till moons shall wax and wane no more.

Chapter Twenty-three

THE FRUITFUL FIG TREE

FOLLOWING THE BINDING OF SATAN and the establishment of the kingdom upon the earth, we have Israel finally and permanently restored to the land. We read:

> In that day sing ye unto her, (Israel, the fig tree, the vine, and the olive tree) A vineyard of red wine.
> I the Lord do keep it; I will water it every moment: lest any hurt it, I will keep it night and day (Isaiah 27:2-3).

This is the promise which God Himself gives here in answer to Israel's confession, that He will restore Israel according to all the promises which He has given. Then there follows, in the sixth verse, a most significant climax to all of this revelation: "He shall cause them that come of Jacob to take root: Israel shall blossom and bud, and fill the face of the world with fruit" (Isaiah 27:6).

Here we have, then, God's own prophetic statement, that following upon these events, the budding of the fig tree, the first Resurrection, the Rapture of the Church, the Second Coming of Christ, the great Tribulation, the binding of Satan, we will have the fruitfulness of the fig tree completely and fully restored. Isaiah is very definite. So that there shall be no mistake whatsover in the interpretation he tells us that: "He shall cause them that come of Jacob to take root: Israel shall blossom and bud, and fill the face of the world with fruit" (Isaiah 27:6).

Here we have the final climax of the work begun when Jesus nineteen hundred years ago, in fulfillment of the prophecy, caused the fig tree to wither away, but only up from the roots. Here we have God keeping the covenant promise with His people, and finally restoring the nation and making them the fruitful vine and the fruit-bearing fig tree, and the restored olive tree of His own delight and of His own pleasure. Before leaving this wonderful passage in the prophecy of Isaiah, we must give just a little thought to the last two verses of this chapter:

> And it shall come to pass in that day, that the Lord shall beat off from the channel of the river unto the stream of Egypt, and ye shall be gathered one by one, O ye children of Israel.
> And it shall come to pass in that day, that the great trumpet shall be blown, and they shall come which were ready to perish in the land of Assyria, and the outcasts in the land of Egypt, and shall worship the Lord in the holy mount at Jerusalem (Isaiah 27:12-13).

This is a remarkable passage which is quite often overlooked by most Bible students. It is a promise that the original covenant which God made with Abraham, Isaac and Jacob, with the nation of Israel, the seed of Jacob, would be ultimately fulfilled. Will you notice carefully the beginning of that twelfth verse: "And it shall come to pass in that day."

"It *shall* come to pass." There is no question about the fulfillment of this. God Jehovah Himself says it *shall* come to pass. It is not a maybe, but it is an absolute promise of something which must come if God is going to retain the integrity of His nature and not be proven to be a liar. Then He goes on to say that it shall come to pass "in that day," and the expression "that day" refers, of course, to that which precedes, the day of the coming of the Lord Jesus Christ and the setting up of the Kingdom upon the earth, in "that day." Isaiah tells us that something will also happen in regard to the *land* of Israel.

He says, "the Lord shall beat off from the channel of the river unto the stream of Egypt." We have here the boundaries of the new restored land in which Israel shall dwell for an everlasting habitation. It is well to remember this carefully.

When we speak of the land of Israel today, most of us think only of the land of Palestine, which is just a little strip of land along the Mediterranean about a hundred miles from north to south and varying from twenty-five to fifty miles in width from the River Jordan to the Mediterranean Sea. This is usually considered the land of Palestine by most people who speak of the land of Israel. When we turn to the original promise of God which He made to Abraham, and confirmed to Isaac and Jacob, we find that the Promised Land, the Holy Land, the land of Israel, the land of Canaan, included a much greater area and territory than is today contained in what we understand to be the land of Palestine. Let me quote to you very briefly from the covenant which God made with Abraham, which was an inviolable and eternal everlasting covenant which cannot be broken in which God gives us the boundaries of the land.

> And I will make of thee a great nation, and I will bless thee, and make thy name great; and thou shalt be a blessing:
> And I will bless them that bless thee, and curse him that curseth thee: and in thee shall all families of the earth be blessed (Genesis 12:2-3).

This, I repeat, was a covenant of grace. There are no conditions that Abraham or his seed must fulfill, but it is absolute promise, wholly independent of the conduct of Abraham or of the nation, of their worth or of their merit, or of their deserts. It is merely a simple covenant and promise of God's grace whereby He promises to make Abraham a great nation, to bless him, to make his name great, to curse all those who curse him and his seed, and to bless all those who bless him and his seed.

Then, in the thirteenth chapter, God adds something to this covenant of grace, and says:

> For all the land which thou seest, to thee will I give it, and to thy seed for ever.
>
> And I will make thy seed as the dust of the earth: so that if a man can number the dust of the earth, then shall thy seed also be numbered (Genesis 13:15-16).

Here then, in addition to the fact that it is a covenant of grace, God says that it will be a union of his seed with the land. As long as the people of the land, Israel, are in the land of Israel, God promises to bless, but when they are separated from their land through the violence of the nations round about, nothing but trouble and war and distress and disappointment will ever come upon the earth. Today the condition of the world with its cold war, with its history of blood shed and the death of millions upon millions of the youth in every age in the strife between the nations can be laid indirectly to the fact that Israel is out of the land and out of the place of blessing among the nations. Only when Israel is completely and fully restored in the land of Palestine by the Lord and not by man, will there ever be peace upon this earth. There is no hope for peace in any other direction or in any other way. It is well for us to remember this, and so God has given us the covenant which tells us definitely that Israel and the land are eternally inseparable.

Then, in the fifteenth chapter of the book of Genesis God adds something else, and this is of a special interest to us now. Here God lays down the boundaries of the land, not as we think of it today in the land of Palestine, but the boundaries according to Scripture itself. In verse 18 of Genesis 15 we read:

> In the same day the Lord made a covenant with Abram, saying, Unto thy seed have I given this land, from the river of Egypt unto the great river, the river Euphrates.

Here then we have the original boundaries set by God Himself. Canaan extends from the river Nile in Egypt and then all the way up north and east to the river Euphrates, up in the middle east and extending from there on to the Mediterranean Sea. This is a vast tract of land, many times larger than the little tract of land which we know as Palestine today. Since Israel has never yet until this day possessed all of this land, but it has been under the domination of other nations, it stands to reason that God must keep His covenant and His promise, if His Word is to be absolutely fulfilled, according to Isaiah twenty-seven, we have God's prophetic statement that He will beat off from the channel of the river of Egypt even unto the great river. Here we have the positive statement that in the future, and we believe in the very near future, the nation of Israel will not only possess the land of Palestine, but all that great tract of land to the north up to the river Euphrates. Israel also, will possess the land to the east all the way through the Sinaitic peninsula and even including northern Africa and part of Egypt up to the Nile River. This is the truth of God's Word. As we see the movements today which are pointing in that direction, we praise God for the fact that His Word still stands and is always true. This is the meaning of the statement in Isaiah: "And it shall come to pass in that day, that the Lord shall beat off from the channel of the river unto the stream of Egypt . . ." (Isaiah 27:12).

A COMPLETE RE-GATHERING

Isaiah goes on and tells us of the re-gathering, not only of a little part of the nation of Israel, but of every last one wherever they may have been scattered, and we read:

> . . . ye shall be gathered one by one, O ye children of Israel.
> And it shall come to pass in that day, that the great trumpet shall be blown, and they shall come which were ready to perish in the land of Assyria, and the outcasts in the land of Egypt, and shall worship the Lord in the holy mount at Jerusalem (Isaiah 27: 12-13).

How we do praise God that we can see the signs and the indications of this day already upon the horizon. We repeat again, the most significant thing in this generation from the standpoint of fulfilled prophecy is the activity among the nation of Israel and their political restoration into the land of Palestine as an independent nation among the peoples of the earth. We believe that this is only a shadow of things to come. It is only the budding of the fig tree, and before very long the Lord is going to take a hand. Then, after the great Tribulation, the awful Time of Jacob's Trouble, God will see to it personally that each one of the remnant is restored in blessing in the land. There will be no suffering, no sorrow, no racial hatred, no persecution, no burning in the fires of affliction, no more rebellion, but they will be blessed of the Lord so that there will be no poverty and no disease, and no harm shall come upon them. For the Lord Himself says His eyes are upon the nation, to deliver them and to redeem them forever and ever. "Pray for the peace of Jerusalem: They shall prosper that love thee."

In closing I want to just refer you to one of hundreds of many, many passages that we might quote from the Scriptures to corroborate the truth, the fact and the absolute certainty that God is going to restore His people again into the land of Israel. I shall give you as representative of these passages, one from the Old Testament and one from the New, with a prayer that many of you who have not seen God's prophetic program may see the clearness of His Hand as He is writing the destiny of the nations through current events today. In the book of Leviticus we read this:

> And I will bring the land into desolation: and your enemies which dwell therein shall be astonished at it.
> And I will scatter you among the heathen, and will draw out a sword after you: and your land shall be desolate, and your cities waste (Leviticus 26: 32-33).

Another quotation:

> And yet for all that, when they be in the land of their enemies, I will not cast them away, neither will I abhor them, to destroy them utterly, and to break my covenant with them: for I am the Lord their God.
>
> But I will for their sakes remember the covenant of their ancestors, whom I brought forth out of the land of Egypt in the sight of the heathen, that I might be their God: I am the Lord (Leviticus 26:44-45).

In the forty-second verse of this same chapter in Leviticus we find this statement:

> Then will I remember my covenant with Jacob, and also my covenant with Isaac, and also my covenant with Abraham will I remember; and I will remember the land.

It is significant that in the promise of God to His people even before they had entered the land of Egypt, He tells them He will not only remember His covenant with Abraham, Isaac and Jacob, but in the end of time will also remember the land. Yes, the Lord has surely spoken, and it shall surely come to pass.

Now for just one quotation taken from the New Testament. In the eleventh chapter of Romans, we read something concerning the future restoration of Israel. After Paul has told us at length about the condition of Israel during this time of dispersion among the nations, he says:

> I say then, Hath God cast away his people? God forbid. For I also am an Israelite, of the seed of Abraham, of the tribe of Benjamin.
>
> God hath not cast away His people which He foreknew (Romans 11:1-2).

This reference is definitely to the people to whom Paul belonged, the nation of Israel, and tells us pointedly that God had not cast them away, even though it might appear so in the eyes of those who know not the Scriptures and the Word of God. Paul also says:

> For I would not, brethren, that ye should be ignorant of this mystery, lest ye should be wise in your own conceits; that blindness in part is happened to Israel, until the fulness of the Gentiles be come in (Romans 11:25).

The word which is the most significant here is "until." That is, the fig tree is withered, but not permanently. The root still remains alive, and the day is coming when it shall blossom and bud and fill the face of the earth with fruit. So this verse which says that "blindness in part is happened to Israel, *Until* the fulness of the Gentiles be come in," can only mean until this present age of the church has been fulfilled and the last member of the body of Christ has been taken in. Then the Rapture of the Church will occur and after that, God will remember Israel again.

> And so all Israel shall be saved: as it is written, There shall come out of Sion the Deliverer, and shall turn away ungodliness from Jacob:
>
> For this is my covenant unto them, when I shall take away their sins (Romans 11:26-27).

May God haste the day. "Pray for the peace of Jerusalem. They shall prosper that love thee."

Printed in the United States of America